Academic
Learning
Series

Microsoft®
Exchange 2000 Server
Implementation and Administration

Lab Manual

PUBLISHED BY
Microsoft Press
A Division of Microsoft Corporation
One Microsoft Way
Redmond, Washington 98052-6399

Library of Congress Cataloging-in-Publication Data
Unkroth, Kay.
      MCSE Training Kit : Microsoft Exchange 2000 Server Implementation and
    Administration / Kay Unkroth.
            p. cm.
       ISBN 0-7356-1028-2
       ISBN 0-7356-1430-x (Academic Learning Series)
       ISBN 0-07-285078-7 (McGraw-Hill Ryerson)
       1. Electronic data processing personnel--Certification. 2. Microsoft
    software--Examinations--Study guides. 3. Microsoft Windows server.   I. Microsoft
    Corporation. II. Title.

    QA76.3 .U54   2000
    005.7'13769--dc21   00-046053

Printed and bound in the United States of America.

1 2 3 4 5 6 7 8 9   QWT   7 6 5 4 3 2

Distributed by McGraw-Hill Ryerson.

A CIP catalogue record for this book is available from the British Library.

Microsoft Press books are available through booksellers and distributors worldwide. For further information about international editions, contact your local Microsoft Corporation office or contact Microsoft Press International directly at fax (425) 706-7329. Visit our Web site at www.microsoft.com/mspress. Send comments to *tkinput@microsoft.com*.

For Microsoft Press   **For Spherion**
Acquisitions Editor: Thomas Pohlmann   **Project Manager:** Daniel Rausch
Project Editor: Julie Miller   **Copy Editor:** Bill McManus
                                                 Technical Editor: Ed Crowley, Jr.
Author: Linda Vittori   **Desktop Publisher:** Arthur Brian Smith

SubAsy Part No. X09-15588
Body Part No. X08-34371

Introduction

This Lab Manual supplements the *ALS: Microsoft Exchange 2000 Server Implementation and Administration* textbook. The labs in this manual are designed to be performed in a classroom environment by a group of students under the supervision of an instructor. This is in contrast to the exercises in the textbook, which are designed to be performed outside the classroom. The labs in this manual and the exercises in the textbook are an essential part of your training. The opportunity to explore the menus, options, and responses will ensure an understanding of the appropriate use of Exchange 2000 Server.

The labs in this manual do not precisely mirror the exercises in the textbook. They are intended to build upon the knowledge and exercises presented in the textbook and offer additional hands-on experience using Exchange 2000 Server. The naming conventions in the Lab Manual are similar to the naming conventions used in the textbook exercises but there are some differences due to the requirement for unique names. Your instructor will explain any differences.

The labs in this manual are performed in a classroom that is configured as an isolated network. The instructor computer is the Domain Name Service (DNS) server for the entire class and it is also a Microsoft Windows 2000 domain controller in the BlueSky-inc-10.com domain. Initially, all student computers are member servers in a workgroup called Workgroup. Upon completion of the labs in this Lab Manual, the classroom will eventually be configured in the multi-forest model and each forest will have a single tree, a single domain, and four servers. Every server will be a Microsoft Windows 2000 domain controller. The lab files required for this course have been copied to the C:\Labfiles folder of your student computer.

The Microsoft Certified Professional (MCP) exams are demanding in both the knowledge and the hands-on experience they require. Students preparing for the Microsoft certification tests can increase their competence by gaining firsthand experience in the implementation and management of Exchange 2000 Server. One of the best ways to become confident in the use of Exchange 2000 Server is to complete all the assigned labs in this manual as well as the exercises in the textbook.

Contents

Lab 1: Creating a Windows 2000 Domain

Objectives

After completing this lab, you will be able to

- Create a new Active Directory forest.
- Create a new Active Directory tree within an existing forest.
- Create a new Active Directory domain.
- Add a new domain controller to an existing domain.

Note Completing this lab will help reinforce your learning from Chapter 2 of the textbook.

Before You Begin

Use the following table for server-to-letter association while performing the lab.

Computer Name	Corresponds To	Domain
Glasgow	A	BlueSky-inc-10.com.uk
Liverpool	B	
London	C	
Manchester	D	
Buenos Aires	A	BlueSky-inc-10.com.sa
Lima	B	
Rio de Janeiro	C	
Santiago	D	
Bordeaux	A	BlueSky-inc-10.com.fr
Nice	B	
Marseille	C	
Paris	D	
Florence	A	BlueSky-inc-10.com.it
Rome	B	
Sicily	C	
Venice	D	
Capetown	A	BlueSky-inc-10.com.af
Dakar	B	
Johannesburg	C	
Nairobi	D	

(continued)

Computer Name	Corresponds To	Domain
Kobe	A	BlueSky-inc-10.com.jp
Kyoto	B	
Sapporo	C	
Tokyo	D	
Canberra	A	BlueSky-inc-10.com.au
Melbourne	B	
Perth	C	
Sydney	D	
Antigua	A	BlueSky-inc-10.com.car
Grenada	B	
Jamaica	C	
Nevis	D	

Estimated time to complete this lab: 60 minutes

Exercise 1
Installing Active Directory Directory
Service on the First Domain Controller

In this exercise, you will log on to your computer as Administrator and use the Active Directory Installation Wizard to install Active Directory on your server.

▶ **To create a new Active Directory domain controller, a new Active Directory domain, and a new Active Directory forest**

Important This procedure should be performed only by the student with the computer name that corresponds to the letter A of the table on pages 1 and 2.

1. Log on to your computer as Administrator with a password of **password**.
2. Click Start, and then click Run.
3. In the Run dialog box, type **dcpromo**, and then click OK to start the Active Directory Installation Wizard.
4. On the Welcome To The Active Directory Installation Wizard screen, click Next.
5. On the Domain Controller Type page, confirm that Domain Controller For A New Domain is selected, and then click Next.
6. On the Create Tree Or Child Domain page, confirm that Create A New Domain Tree is selected, and then click Next.
7. On the Create Or Join Forest page, confirm that Create A New Forest Of Domain Trees is selected, and then click Next.
8. On the New Domain Name page, in the Full DNS Name For New Domain text box, type **<Domain Name>** (where <Domain Name> corresponds to the domain name for your computer in the lab table), and then click Next.
9. If you receive a warning that the default NetBIOS domain name resulted in a name conflict, click OK.
10. On the NetBIOS Domain Name wizard screen, change the Domain NetBIOS Name to **BLUESKY<Domain Name>**, and then click Next.
11. On the Database And Log Locations page, click Next to accept the default locations.
12. On the Shared System Volume page, click Next to accept the default location.
13. On the Permissions page, select Permissions Compatible Only With Windows 2000 Servers, and then click Next.

14. On the Directory Services Restore Mode Administrator Password page, type **password** in the Password and Confirm Password text boxes, and then click Next.

15. Review your options on the Summary page, and then click Next.

    The installation of Active Directory will begin. This process can take several minutes.

16. When the Completing The Active Directory Installation Wizard screen appears, click Finish.

17. When prompted, restart your computer.

Exercise 2
Installing Active Directory Directory
Service on the Remaining Domain Controllers

In this exercise, you will install Active Directory on your computer to create a new domain controller in an existing domain.

Important Exercise 1 must be completed by the student with the computer name that corresponds to the letter A in the table on pages 1 and 2 before the remaining students begin this exercise.

▶ **To create a domain controller in an existing domain**

Important This procedure should be performed only by the students with computer names that correspond to the letters B, C, and D of the table on pages 1 and 2.

---

1. Log on to your computer as Administrator with a password of **password**.
2. Click Start, and then click Run.
3. In the Run dialog box, type **dcpromo**, and then click OK to start the Active Directory Installation Wizard.
4. On the Welcome To The Active Directory Installation Wizard screen, click Next.
5. On the Domain Controller Type page, click Additional Domain Controller For An Existing Domain, and then click Next.
6. On the Network Credentials page, type **Administrator** for User Name, **password** for Password, and **<Domain Name>** for the Domain (where <Domain Name> corresponds to the domain name for your computer in the lab table), and then click Next.
7. On the Additional Domain Controller page, type **<Domain Name>**, and then click Next.
8. On the Database And Log Locations page, click Next to accept the default settings.
9. On the Shared System Volume page, click Next to accept the default settings.
10. On the Directory Services Restore Mode Administrator Password page, under Password and Confirm Password, type **password**, then click Next.
11. Confirm the settings, then click Next to start the installation of Active Directory. This will take a few minutes.

12. Click Finish.

13. You will be prompted to restart your computer now or restart it later. Click Restart Now.

Exercise 3
Confirming the Installation of Active Directory Directory Service

In this exercise, you will use the Active Directory Users and Computers MMC snap-in to confirm that the installation of Active Directory on your computer was successful.

▶ **To confirm the status of your computer as a domain controller**

1. Once all the computers in your group have finished rebooting, log on to your assigned domain as Administrator with a password of **password**.

2. Click Start, and then click Run.

3. In the Run dialog box, type **mmc**, and then click OK to start the Microsoft Management Console (MMC).

4. Open the Console menu, and select Add/Remove Snap-In.

5. In the Add/Remove Snap-In dialog box, click Add.

6. In the Add Standalone Snap-In dialog box, click Active Directory Users And Computers, click Add, and then click Close.

7. In the Add/Remove Snap-In dialog box, click OK. In the console tree, expand the Active Directory Users And Computers node.

8. Expand your domain and then select the Domain Controllers container.

   Do you see the name of your computer in the contents pane?

   _____Yes_____

   Do you see the names of the other computers that are part of your domain?

   _____Yes_____

Note If you don't see the other domain controllers in the contents pane, press F5 to refresh your screen. Sometimes it takes time to see all the domain controllers.

---

9. Open the Console menu and select Save As to display the Save As dialog box.

10. From the Save In list box, select C:\Documents and Settings\ All Users\Desktop.

11. In the File Name box, type **<Your First Names> Console** (for example, if your name is Gary, type Garys Console).

12. Click Save.

Note By saving your console under C:\Documents and Settings\All Users\ Desktop, you will have access to your customized console for the duration of the class regardless of how you are logged on to your computer.

13. Close your console and log off your computer.

Lab 2: Preparing for an Exchange 2000 Server Installation

Objectives

After completing this lab, you will be able to

- Prepare an Active Directory forest for a Microsoft Exchange 2000 installation using ForestPrep.
- Confirm that Active Directory directory service has been extended to prepare for an Exchange 2000 installation.

Note Completing this lab will help reinforce your learning from Chapter 4 of the textbook.

Estimated time to complete this lab: 30 minutes

Exercise 1
Running ForestPrep

In this exercise, you will log on to your computer as Administrator and use the Microsoft Exchange 2000 Installation Wizard to prepare your forest for an Exchange 2000 installation.

▶   **To extend the Active Directory schema using ForestPrep**

Important This procedure should be performed only by the student who corresponds to Server in the table on pages 1 and 2.

---

1. Log on to your computer as Administrator using a password of **password**.
2. Click Start, and then click Run.
3. In the Run dialog box, type **Washington\exch\setup /forestprep**, and then click OK.
4. On the Welcome wizard screen of the Microsoft Exchange 2000 Installation Wizard, click Next.
5. On the End-User License Agreement wizard screen, select I Agree to accept the licensing agreement, and then click Next.
6. Accept the 25-digit CD key by clicking Next, or type in the CD key provided by the instructor.
7. On the Component Selection wizard screen, confirm that ForestPrep is entered next to Microsoft Exchange 2000, note the installation location, and then click Next.

Note If you don't see ForestPrep, that usually indicates that you made a typographical error in the setup command. Exit Setup, and begin again at Step 3. Failing to start over will install Exchange 2000 Server using a Typical installation.

---

8. On the Installation Type wizard screen, confirm that Create A New Exchange Organization is selected, and then click Next.
9. On the Organization Name wizard screen, under Organization Name, type the organization name assigned by your instructor, and then click Next.
10. On the Exchange 2000 Administrator Account wizard screen, confirm that <Domain Name>\Administrator is entered (for example, if your domain name is Bluesky-inc-10.com.uk, confirm that Bluesky-inc-10.com.uk\ Administrator is entered), and then click Next.
11. The Component Progress wizard screen shows that the Active Directory schema is being updated, which may take up to 20 minutes. When the update is complete, click Next.
12. On the Completing The Microsoft Exchange 2000 Installation Wizard screen, click Finish.

Exercise 2
Confirming the Installation of the
Exchange 2000 Schema Extensions

In this exercise, all students will install the Active Directory Schema snap-in and use it to view the Exchange 2000 schema extensions.

▶ **To confirm the installation of Exchange 2000 schema extensions**

1. Click Start, and then click Run.

2. In the Run dialog box, type **regsvr32 SCHMMGMT.DLL**, and then click OK.

3. Click OK to close the Success dialog box.

4. Open the Microsoft Management Console (MMC) you created on your desktop.

5. Open the Console menu, and select Add/Remove Snap-In.

6. In the Add/Remove Snap-In dialog box, click Add.

7. In the Add Standalone Snap-In dialog box, select Active Directory Schema, click Add, and then click Close.

8. In the Add/Remove Snap-In dialog box, click OK.

9. In the console tree, expand Active Directory Schema, and then select Classes.

10. In the details pane, scroll down until you see the extensions that begin with msExch, confirming that the schema has been extended.

Note If you don't see the extensions, directory replication may not have occurred on your server yet.

---

11. Close your console and log off your computer.

Lab 3: Installing Exchange 2000 Server

Objectives

After completing this lab, you will be able to

- Prepare the domain to install by using DomainPrep.
- Install Microsoft Exchange 2000 Server on your computer.
- Confirm the Exchange 2000 Server installation.

Note Completing this lab will help reinforce your learning from Chapter 5 of the textbook.

Estimated time to complete this lab: 60 minutes

Exercise 1
Preparing the Domain for an
Exchange 2000 Installation Using DomainPrep

In this exercise, you will log on to your computer as Administrator and use the Microsoft Exchange 2000 Installation Wizard to prepare your forest for an Exchange 2000 installation. You will use DomainPrep to create the domain local and domain global groups required by the Exchange 2000 services for authentication.

▶   **To prepare the domain for an Exchange 2000 Server installation**

Important This procedure should be performed only by one student in each domain.

---

1. Log on to your domain as Administrator with a password of **password**.
2. Click Start, and then click Run.
3. In the Open dialog box, type **Washington\exch\setup /domainprep**, and then click OK.
4. On the Welcome To The Microsoft Exchange 2000 Installation Wizard screen, click Next.
5. In the End-User License Agreement dialog box, select I Agree, and then click Next.
6. On the Product Identification page, accept the 25-digit CD key by clicking Next, or type in the CD key provided by the instructor.
7. On the Component Selection wizard screen, confirm that DomainPrep is entered next to Microsoft Exchange 2000 under Action, and then click Next.

Note If you don't see DomainPrep, that usually indicates that you made a typographical error in the setup command. Exit Setup, and begin again at Step 3. Failure to start over will install Exchange 2000 Server using a Typical installation.

---

8. When you receive an insecure domain error, click OK.
9. On the Completing The Microsoft Exchange 2000 Wizard screen, click Finish.

Exercise 2
Installing Exchange 2000 Server

In this exercise, you will install Exchange 2000 Server and customize your installation by selecting to install the Instant Messaging component.

▶   **To install Instant Messaging**

Important This procedure should be completed by all students.

---

1. If you're not already logged on to your domain, log on now as Administrator with a password of **password**.

2. Click Start, and then click Run.

3. In the Open dialog box, type **\\Washington\exch\setup**, and then click OK.

4. On the Welcome To The Microsoft Exchange 2000 Installation Wizard screen, click Next.

5. In the End-User License Agreement dialog box, select I Agree, and then click Next.

6. On the Product Identification wizard screen, accept the 25-digit CD key by clicking Next, or type in the CD key provided by the instructor .

7. On the Component Selection wizard screen, select Custom in the Action list for Microsoft Exchange 2000.

8. Verify that Install is selected in the Action list for Microsoft Exchange Messaging and Collaboration Services.

9. Verify that Install is selected in the Action list for Microsoft Exchange System Management Tools.

10. Select Install in the Action list for Microsoft Exchange Instant Messaging Service, and then click Next.

11. On the Licensing Agreement wizard screen, select I Agree, and then click Next.

12. Review the installation options and verify that you are installing the three components:

    ■ Microsoft Exchange Messaging and Collaboration Services

    ■ Microsoft Exchange System Management Tools

    ■ Microsoft Exchange Instant Messaging Service

13. If everything is correct, click Next.

    Setup will copy the necessary files and will install Exchange 2000 Server.

14. On the Completing The Microsoft Exchange 2000 Installation Wizard screen, click Finish.

Exercise 3
Confirming the Exchange 2000 Server Installation

In this exercise, you will confirm the installation of Exchange 2000 Server by viewing the Server object in Exchange System Manager and by checking the log file created by Setup.

▶   **To confirm the installation of Exchange 2000 Server**

Important All students should complete this procedure.

---

1. Double-click the MMC you created on your desktop.
2. In the management console, open the Console menu and select Add/Remove Snap-In.
3. In the Add/Remove Snap-In dialog box, click Add.
4. In the Add Standalone Snap-In dialog box, select Services, and then click Add.
5. In the Services dialog box, confirm that Local Computer is selected, and then click Finish.
6. In the Add Standalone Snap-In dialog box, select Exchange System, and then click Add.
7. In the Change Domain Controller dialog box, click OK.
8. Click Close to close the Add Standalone Snap-In dialog box.
9. In the Add/Remove Snap-In dialog box, click OK.
10. Under Console Root, select Services.
11. In the details pane, scroll down to the services that begin with Microsoft Exchange to view the services that have been installed. (You might need to widen the Name column.) Notice in the Startup Type column the services that are configured to start automatically or manually or that are disabled.
12. Expand your assigned country's Blue Sky Airlines (Exchange) and select Servers.
13. Confirm that your server is listed.
14. Close your console, and click Yes when prompted to save your settings.

Lab 4: Analyzing an Upgrade from Exchange Server 5.5 to Exchange 2000 Server

Objectives

After completing this lab, you will be able to

- Describe the steps necessary to upgrade a Microsoft Windows NT 4 server with Microsoft Exchange 5.5 Server to a Microsoft Windows 2000 server with Microsoft Exchange 2000 Server.

- Describe the steps required to change from an Exchange 2000 mixed mode environment to an Exchange 2000 native mode environment.

- Describe post-upgrade considerations.

Note Completing this lab will help reinforce your learning from Chapter 6 of the textbook.

Estimated time to complete the lab: 30 minutes

Exercise 1
Upgrading from an Exchange 5.5 Server
to an Exchange 2000 Server

In this exercise, you will work as a group to plan for an upgrade to Exchange 2000 Server. Your instructor will facilitate, but this is your brainstorming session.

Scenario

You are part of the Exchange design and deployment team for your company, Blue Sky Airlines. You are preparing to upgrade from Exchange 5.5 Server on Windows NT 4 Server to Exchange 2000 Server on Windows 2000 Server. You have confirmed that all of your hardware is on the Hardware Compatibility List for Windows 2000 Server and that your servers fulfill all the resource requirements to meet the needs of your organization. You currently have a single Windows NT 4 domain model, and the name of your primary domain controller (PDC) is PDC-1, as shown in Figure 4.1. You have one Exchange 5.5 site with one server named EX01, as shown in Figure 4.2.

PDC-1

EX01

Figure 4.1
Server running Windows NT 4 with
Server Pack 6 and Exchange 5.5

Figure 4.2
Server running Windows NT 4 with Service
Pack 6

1. Based on the preceding information, outline the considerations and the initial steps you must take before upgrading your company from Exchange 5.5 Server to Exchange 2000 Server.

    _____

    _____

    _____

    _____

    _____

    _____

    _____

    _____

2. What are the considerations and the required steps to upgrade the Exchange 5.5 server to Exchange 2000 Server?

    _____

    _____

    _____

    _____

    _____

3. What must be done to convert your company to an all-Exchange 2000 environment?

    _____

    _____

    _____

    _____

    _____

4. What should you do after the upgrade and the mode conversion are complete?

    _____

    _____

    _____

    _____

Lab 5: Describing Cluster Service Components

Objectives

After completing this lab, you will be able to

- Describe the components of the Microsoft Windows 2000 Cluster service.
- Describe the relationship the Cluster service components have with one another.

Note Completing this lab will help reinforce your learning from Chapter 7 of the textbook.

Estimated time to complete this lab: 30 minutes

Exercise 1
Determining the Relationship Cluster Service Components Have with One Another

In this exercise, you will work as a group to describe the components of the Cluster service and the relationship the components have with one another. You will be assigned a number by the instructor that corresponds to a numbered term on the following worksheet. You will find the definition for your assigned term and then will be called upon to present the information to the class. You will use the white board to show how your component is used by the Cluster service. You can use your worksheet to record the information you receive from the other students.

Windows 2000 Cluster Service

Component Number	Component Name	Component Description
1	Node Manager	
2	Communications Manager	
3	Resource Monitor	
4	Resource Manager	
5	Failover Manager	
6	Configuration Database Manager	
7	Quorum disk	
8	Checkpoint Manager	
9	Global Update Manager	
10	Log Manager	
11	Sponsor	
12	Event Processor	

Lab 6: Installing Outlook 2000

Objectives

After completing this lab, you will be able to

■ Install Microsoft Outlook 2000.

Note Completing this lab will help reinforce your learning from Chapter 8 of the textbook.

Estimated time to complete this lab: 30 minutes

Exercise 1
Installing Outlook 2000

In this exercise, you will install Outlook 2000 on your computer by running Setup while connected to the instructor's server.

▶   **To install Outlook 2000**

1. If you're not already logged on to your domain, log on now as Administrator with a password of **password**.

2. Click Start, and then click Run.

3. In the Run dialog box, type **Washington\Outlook\setup.exe**.

4. On the Welcome To Microsoft Outlook 2000 wizard screen, type **Administrator** for the User Name, type **Blue Sky Airlines** for the Organization, and type the 25-digit product key provided by your instructor. Click Next.

5. On the Microsoft Outlook 2000 End-User License Agreement wizard screen, select the I Accept The Terms In The License Agreement option, and then click Next.

6. On the Microsoft Outlook 2000: Ready To Install wizard screen, select Customize.

7. On the Microsoft Outlook 2000 Installation Location wizard screen, notice that you can select where you want to install Outlook. Accept the default location, and then click Next.

8. On the Microsoft Outlook 2000: Selecting Features wizard screen, click on the node for Microsoft Outlook For Windows and notice the features selected for installation.

9. Click the drop-down menu next to the Help option, and notice that you have the option to run Outlook from your computer or from a CD. Accept the defaults.

10. Click Install Now.

11. When the Installing Microsoft Outlook 2000 progress bar shows that the installation has completed, click OK to acknowledge that Microsoft Outlook 2000 Setup completed successfully.

12. If the Installer Information wizard screen appears, click Yes to restart your system.

13. Log on to your domain as Administrator with a password of **password**.

14. The Outlook icon on the desktop indicates that Outlook has been installed successfully.

Lab 7: Creating an Outlook 2000 MAPI Profile

Objectives

After completing this lab, you will be able to

- Create a user account with permissions to manage Microsoft Exchange 2000 Server.

- Create a logon script to automatically generate a Messaging Application Programming Interface (MAPI) profile at logon.

Note Completing this lab will help reinforce your learning from Chapter 9 of the textbook.

Estimated time to complete this lab: 40 minutes

Exercise 1
Creating a Personal Windows 2000 User Account

In this exercise, you will create a user account with permission to administer Exchange 2000 Server, to use for the duration of this course.

▶ **To create a Microsoft Windows 2000 user account**

1. Log on to your computer as Administrator with a password of **password**.

2. Double-click the Microsoft Management Console (MMC) icon that you created in Lab 1.

3. In the console tree, expand Active Directory Users And Computers.

4. Expand your BlueSky domain.

5. Right-click the Users container.

6. Select New, and then select User.

7. In the New Object – User dialog box, type your First Name, your Last Name, and your User Logon Name using your first name and first initial of your last name, and then click Next.

8. On the next wizard screen, under Password and Confirm Password, type **password**, and then click Next.

9. On the next wizard screen, confirm that Create An Exchange Mailbox is selected on your server in the First Storage Group, and then click Next.

10. On the last wizard screen, confirm that your settings are correct and click Finish.

11. Double-click on your user object in the Users container, and select the Member Of property sheet.

12. Click Add and select Domain Admins. If you first click the Name column heading, the list will sort alphabetically.

13. Click Add, and then click OK twice to close the user property page.

Exercise 2
Using a Logon Script to Generate a MAPI Profile

In this exercise, you will modify a profile descriptor file and use it in a logon script to automatically generate a MAPI profile when you log on as your new user account. You will then open Outlook and send a message to your partner.

▶ **To automatically generate a MAPI profile**

1. In Windows Explorer, right-click on C:\Labfiles\Outlook\outlook.prf, select Open With, and then select Notepad.

2. Scroll down to Section 1 – Profile defaults, and confirm that under the [General] section you see

   Custom=1

   ProfileName=Microsoft Outlook

   DefaultProfile=Yes

   OverwriteProfile=Yes

   Default Store=Service2

3. Change the ProfileName entry from Microsoft Outlook to **Blue Sky Airlines**.

   What service does the Service2 entry refer to? How can you tell?

   _____

   _____

4. Scroll down to Section 2 – Services In Profile, and under [Service List], place a semicolon in front of both Service4 and Service5 so that those options don't become part of the profile.

5. Scroll down to Section 4 – Default Values for each service, and under [Service2], change HomeServer=<Exchange Server> to **HomeServer=<Server Name>** (for example, if your server name is Washington, change HomeServer=<Exchange Server> to HomeServer=Washington).

6. In this same section, under the HomeServer entry, add the entry **MailboxName=%User Name%**. By adding this entry in the variable format, the credentials of the user currently logged on will be used for name resolution.

7. On the File menu, click Save and then click Exit.

8. In Windows Explorer, navigate to C:\Winnt\Sysvol\sysvol\<Domain Name>\scripts.

9. Create a new text document in the contents pane named **PROFGEN.BAT** with the following text: **"C:\Program Files\Common Files\system\mapi\ 1033\nt\ newprof.exe" -p C:\LabFiles\Outlook\outlook.prf**.

Important Be sure to use the quotes around the path to NEWPROF.EXE. Don't forget about the problems the spaces will cause.

---

10. From the File menu, click Save and click Exit.

11. In the MMC, using the Active Directory Users And Computers snap-in, double-click on the user account you created in the Users folder.

12. Select the Profile property sheet and, in the Logon Script text box, type **PROFGEN.BAT**, and then click OK.

Important You have just modified the profile descriptor file, written a logon script to use NEWPROF.EXE to read your settings, and instructed Windows to run the script the next time you log on.

---

13. Close all programs, log off, and log on as your new account.

14. When the Windows 2000 Configure Your Server application opens, deselect the Show This Screen At Startup check box, and then close the application.

15. Right-click on the Outlook icon on your desktop, and select Properties.

    What services have been added to your profile?

    _____

    _____

16. Click the Show Profiles button.

    What is the name of the profile?

    _____

17. Close the Mail dialog box.

18. Double-click on Microsoft Outlook.

19. If you see the Windows Installer window, wait until it has completed configuring Outlook. When the User Name dialog box appears, click OK to accept the Name and Initials.

20. If you are asked whether you would like to register Outlook as the default manager for Mail, News, and Contacts, click Yes.

21. When the Welcome To Microsoft Outlook Office Assistant icon appears, click Start Using Microsoft Outlook.

22. Right-click on Clippit, and select Hide (unless you like having it visible).

23. Compose a new message, and send it to the other students in your domain.

24. Return to the Active Directory Users And Computers MMC snap-in, and remove PROFGEN.BAT from the Profile property sheet.

Exercise 3 (Optional)
Using a Group Policy Object (GPO) to
Generate a MAPI Profile

Only one student in each domain should create the group policy object. After the GPO has been assigned, all students can log on and have a MAPI profile automatically generated for them in a way similar to the way it was created, using a logon script. Before you begin this exercise, all existing profiles should be removed from Outlook, and you should confirm that the PROFGEN.BAT file has been removed from everyone's Profile property sheet.

▶ **To generate a MAPI profile using a GPO**

Important Steps 1–9 should be performed by only one student in each domain.

1. Open the MMC, and expand Active Directory Users And Computers.
2. Right-click on your <Domain Name> (for example, BlueSky-inc-10.com.uk), and select Properties.
3. On the Group Policy property sheet, select Default Domain Policy and click Edit.
4. Expand User Configuration, expand Windows Settings, and select Scripts.
5. In the right pane, double-click Logon.
6. Click Add, browse to My Network Places\Entire Network\Microsoft Windows Network\<Domain Name>\<Server Name>\SYSVOL\<Domain Name>\scripts, select PROFGEN.BAT, and click Open.
7. Click OK to close the Add A Script dialog box, and click OK again to close the Logon Properties dialog box.
8. Close the group policy object, and click OK to close the Properties dialog box for your domain.
9. Close all programs, and log off your computer.

Important All students can perform steps 10–16.

10. Log on to your computer with your user account and password.
11. Double-click the Outlook icon on your desktop.
12. Does Outlook open without being prompted to create a profile? Why?

_____

_____

13. From the menu bar, select Tools, and then select Services.

   What information services have been set up in this profile?

   _____

   _____

14. Click the Copy button.

   What is the name of this profile? Why is it called that?

   _____

   _____

15. Click Cancel to close the Copy Information Service dialog box, and click OK to close the Services box.

16. Close Outlook.

Important Steps 16–20 should be performed by only one student in the domain.

---

17. Reopen your MMC, and in Active Directory Users And Computers, select the Group Policy page in the Properties dialog box for your domain.

18. Expand User Configuration, expand Windows Settings, select Scripts, and double-click Logon.

19. Select the GPO that you created, and click Remove.

20. Click OK to close the Logon Properties dialog box. Close the Group Policy window, and then click OK to close the Properties dialog box for your domain.

21. Close your MMC.

22. Log off the computer.

Lab 8: Testing an RPC Connection with RPCPing

Objective

After completing this lab, you will be able to

■ Test a remote procedure call (RPC) connection between a client and a server.

Note Completing this lab will reinforce your learning from Chapter 10 of the textbook.

Estimated time to complete this lab: 10 minutes

Exercise 1
Testing a Client/Server RPC Connection

This exercise should be performed with a partner in your own domain. One student will run the server version of RPCPing, and the other student will run the 32-bit client version of RPCPing. The purpose of this exercise is to demonstrate how simple the RPCPing utility is to use when managing a Novell network and planning to deploy Microsoft Exchange 2000 Server.

▶ **To install the server version of RPCPing**

Important This procedure should be performed by the student representing the server.

---

1. Log on to your server with your user account and password.
2. Click the Start button, point to Run, and, in the Run dialog box, type **C:\LabFiles\RPCping\rpings.exe**.
3. Click OK, and notice that all the installed protocols are set for use.
4. Don't exit the program.

▶ **To install the client version of RPCPing**

Important This procedure should be performed by the student representing the client.

---

1. Log on to your server with your user account and password.
2. Click the Start button, point to Run, and, in the Run dialog box, type **C:\LabFiles\RPCping\rpingc.exe**.
3. Click OK.
4. In the Exchange Server dialog box, type the name of your partner's server.
5. Click Start.

   Was a connection made? Why or why not?

   _____

6. In the Protocol Sequence list box, select IPX/SPX from the drop-down menu.
7. Click Start.

   Was a connection made? Why or why not?

   _____

   _____

8. Click OK three times to close the three error boxes.

9. Click Exit.

10. The student representing the server should type **@q** to exit RPCPing.

Lab 9: Configuring Internet Protocols Using Outlook Express

Objectives

After completing this lab, you will be able to

- Configure Microsoft Outlook Express as an IMAP4 client.
- Use the Lightweight Directory Access Protocol (LDAP) to perform an Active Directory lookup.
- Configure Outlook Express as a POP3 client.
- Access e-mail using HTTP with Microsoft Outlook Web Access (OWA).

Note Completing this lab will reinforce your learning from Chapter 11 of the textbook.

Estimated time to complete this lab: 30 minutes

Exercise 1
Configuring Outlook Express as an IMAP4 Client

In this exercise, you will configure an IMAP e-mail account in Outlook Express and use it to gain access to e-mail and private and public folders. You will use LDAP to look up your user account in Active Directory directory service, and you will use the address found in the LDAP query to send yourself a message. After you read your e-mail as an IMAP4 client, you will use OWA to confirm that your e-mail messages are still on the server.

► **To configure Outlook Express as an IMAP4 client**

1. Log on to your computer with your user account and password.

2. Click Start, and on the Programs menu, select Outlook Express. This will launch the Internet Connection Wizard.

3. Click Yes when you are asked whether you want to make Outlook Express your default mail client.

4. On the Your Name wizard screen, enter your name under Display Name, and then click Next.

5. Confirm that I Already Have An E-Mail Address That I'd Like To Use is selected, enter the SMTP address for your user account in the E-Mail Address field, and then click Next.

6. On the E-Mail Server Names wizard screen, select IMAP from the list box, type the name of your server in both the Incoming Mail and Outgoing Mail text boxes, and then click Next.

7. In the Internet Mail Logon dialog box, confirm that your logon name is in the Account Name text box, type **password** in the Password text box, and then click Next.

8. Click Finish.

9. In the Internet Accounts dialog box, select the Mail tab, select your mail account, and then click the Properties button.

10. In the General tab, confirm that the name under Mail Account is <Server Name>-IMAP. (For example, if your server name is Washington, the name should be Washington-IMAP.) Click OK, and then click Close.

11. When asked whether you would like to download folders from the server, select Yes.

    You will see a list of folders, including your Inbox and all of your private folders and public folders, including the public folder Internet Newsgroups.

12. Double-click on some of the folders in the list, and then click OK.

Notice that you have two folders: one named Local Folders and one named <Server Name>-IMAP. The <Server Name>-IMAP folder should contain all of your private folders and the public folders that you selected. Notice that you can read messages that are in the public folders and your Inbox.

▶ **To send a message using Outlook Express as an IMAP client**

1. Click New Mail in the toolbar.

2. Click the To button, and, in the Select Recipients dialog box, click Find.

3. In the Find People dialog box, from the Look In list box, select Active Directory.

4. In the Name text box, type your first name, and then click Find Now.

   You should now see your name in the lower part of the Find People dialog box.

5. Select your name, click the Add To Address Book button, and then click OK.

6. Repeat step 5 to include the addresses of the other members of your domain.

7. Click OK to return to the Find People dialog box, and then click the To button.

8. In the Select Recipients dialog box, click OK.

9. In the Subject field of the new message, type **This is from my IMAP client**, and then click Send.

10. Click on the Inbox under Local Folders, and then click on the Inbox under <Server Name>-IMAP.

    Do you see your message in the Inbox under Local Folders or under <Server Name>-IMAP? Why or why not?

    _____

    _____

▶ **To use OWA to confirm that your e-mail messages remained on your server after using your IMAP account**

1. Launch Microsoft Internet Explorer, and, in the Address text box, type **<Server Name>/exchange**. (For example, if your server is named Washington, type **Washington/exchange**.)

   Is your IMAP message in your Inbox? Why or why not?

   _____

2. Close Internet Explorer.

Exercise 2
Configuring Outlook Express as a POP3 Client

Now that you have seen how IMAP4 operates, in this exercise, you will configure a POP3 account using Outlook Express and make a comparison between the two Internet client-access protocols.

▶ **To configure Outlook Express as a POP3 client**

1. Log on to your computer with your user account and password.

2. Click Start, and, on the Programs menu, select Outlook Express.

3. On the Tools menu, select Accounts.

4. In the Internet Accounts dialog box, click Add, and then select Mail.

5. On the Your Name wizard screen, confirm that your name appears under Display Name, and then click Next.

6. Confirm that I Already Have An E-Mail Address That I'd Like To Use is selected, enter the SMTP address for your user account in the E-Mail Address field, and then click Next.

7. On the E-Mail Server Names wizard screen, select POP3 from the list box, type the name of your server in both the Incoming Mail and Outgoing Mail text boxes, and then click Next.

8. In the Internet Mail Logon dialog box, confirm that your name is in the Account Name text field, type **password** in the Password text field, and then click Next.

9. Click Finish.

10. In the Internet Accounts dialog box, select the Mail tab, select the <SERVERNAME>-POP3 account name (for example, if your server name is Washington, select <WASHINGTON>-POP3), and then select Properties.

11. On the General tab, change the name of the account from <Server Name> to **<Server Name>-POP3**. Click OK, and then click Close.

12. Click the POP3 mail account, select the Set As Default button, and then click Close.

    Do you see an entry for <Server Name>-POP3 under Folders in Outlook Express? Why or why not?

    _____

    _____

    Do you have an option to include private or public folders in the POP3 account? Why or why not?

    _____

    _____

13. Select Sent Items under the IMAP account, and then select Sent Items under Local Folders.

    Do you see the same items? Why or why not?

    _____

    _____

▶   **To send a message using Outlook Express as a POP3 client**

1. Create a new e-mail message, type **This is from my POP3 client**, and then send the message to your user account.

2. Select Inbox under Local Folders. The message you sent in step 1 should be there. If it isn't, click the Send/Recv button on the toolbar or press CTRL+M to retrieve all e-mail.

3. After you see the message under Local Folders, select Inbox under the IMAP account. Are any messages there? Why or why not?

   _____

   _____

▶   **To use OWA to confirm that your e-mail messages did not remain on your server after using your POP3 account**

1. Launch Internet Explorer, and, in the Address text box, type **<Server Name>/exchange**. (For example, if your server name is Washington, type Washington/exchange.)

   Are your IMAP and POP3 messages in your Inbox? Why or why not?

   _____

   _____

2. Close Internet Explorer.

3. Close Outlook Express.

Lab 10: Configuring NNTP Using Outlook Express

Objectives

After completing this lab, you will be able to

- Create a newsgroup using Exchange System Manager.
- Configure Microsoft Outlook Express to access the newsgroup you created on your server.

Note Completing this lab will reinforce your learning from Chapter 11 of the textbook.

Estimated time to complete this lab: 20 minutes

Exercise 1
Creating a Newsgroup

In this exercise, you will create a newsgroup by using Exchange System Manager. Once that is completed, you will configure Outlook Express as a Network News Transfer Protocol (NNTP) client and send a post to your newly created newsgroup.

▶ **To create a newsgroup using Exchange System Manager**

1. Log on to your computer with your user account and password.

2. Launch the Microsoft Management Console (MMC) located on your desktop.

3. Expand Exchange System Manager, expand Servers, expand your server, expand Protocols, expand NNTP, and then expand Default NNTP Virtual Server.

4. Select Newsgroups, right-click it, point to New, and select Newsgroup.

5. On the first New Newsgroup wizard screen, under Name, type **<Your Alias>** (for example, if your alias is Admin, type Admin), and then click Next.

6. On the second New Newsgroup wizard screen, under Description, type **<Your Aliass> Newsgroups** (for example, Admins Newsgroups).

    Pretty Name is an alias that is displayed for the client.

Note Avoid the use of periods in your alias name to prevent the creation of sub-newsgroups.

---

7. Click Finish.

8. Once again, select Newsgroups, right-click it, point to New, and select Newsgroup.

9. On the first New Newsgroup wizard screen, type **<your alias>.hobbies**, and click Next.

10. On the second New Newsgroup wizard screen, under Description, type **Talk about your Hobbies**, and click Finish.

    Notice that your newsgroups are listed in the contents pane of the Newsgroups container.

11. Close your MMC.

▶ **To connect to your newsgroup using Outlook Express**

1. Click the Start button, point to Programs, and select Outlook Express.

2. Open the Tools menu, and select Accounts.

3. In the Internet Accounts dialog box, click Add, and then select News.

4. On the first wizard screen, confirm that your name is in the Display name field, and click Next.

5. On the second wizard screen, confirm that your SMTP address is correct, and then click Next.

6. On the Internet News Server Names wizard screen, under News (NNTP) Server, type the name of your server, click Next, and then click Finish.

7. In the Internet Accounts dialog box, click on the News tab and click the Properties button for the account you just created.

8. On the General tab, change the name of the account from <server name> to <server name>-Newsgroups (for example, if your server name is Washington, change Washington to Washington-Newsgroups). Click OK, and then click Close.

9. When asked whether you would like to download newsgroups from the news account you added, click Yes.

   You will see the newsgroups you created on your server in the Newsgroup Subscriptions dialog box.

10. While holding down the Ctrl key, select your newsgroups, and then click Subscribe. Click OK.

    You should see <server name>-News with the newsgroups you subscribed to listed in the Folders pane of Outlook Express.

11. Click your newsgroup in the Folders pane of Outlook Express, and then click the New Post icon in the toolbar.

12. In the Subject line of the new message, type the name of your favorite hobby, type a short message about your hobby, and then click Send.

13. You will receive a dialog box (it may not appear immediately) informing you that your post is being sent to the news server. Click OK.

14. Wait one minute, select your newsgroup, and then press F5 to refresh your screen. Your message should appear in your newsgroup.

▶ **To access your newsgroup using Microsoft Internet Explorer**

1. Launch Internet Explorer, and, in the Address line, type **<Server Name>/exchange** (for example, if your server name is Washington, type Washington/exchange).

2. Click the Folders option in the Outlook Bar located on the left side of the Internet Explorer window.

3. Expand the Public Folders container.

   Can you access your newsgroup as well as the other newsgroups in your organization using Internet Explorer?

---

4. Close Internet Explorer.

5. Close Outlook Express.

Lab 11: Exploring the Extensions for the Exchange System Manager Snap-In

Objectives

After completing this lab, you will be able to

- Add the Exchange System Manager snap-in to the console and observe installed components.
- View the results after removing the extensions for the Exchange System Manager snap-in.
- Describe the purpose of snap-in extensions.

Note Completing this lab will reinforce your learning from Chapter 12 of the textbook.

Estimated time to complete this lab: 30 minutes

Exercise 1
Examining the Effects of Removing Extensions for the Exchange System Manager MMC Snap-In

In this exercise, you will open a Microsoft Management Console (MMC) window and add the Exchange System Manager snap-in to the console. You will view administrative capabilities using the snap-in. Then you will remove all the extensions from the Exchange System Manager snap-in and see the effect this has on your administrative capabilities. Next you will replace some of the extensions that you removed earlier and view the results. Finally, you will add the remaining extensions back into the Exchange System Manager snap-in to restore full administrative capabilities.

▶ **To add the Exchange System Manager snap-in to your console and observe the installed components**

1. Log on to your computer with your user account and password.

2. Click Start, and then click Run.

3. In the Run dialog box, type **mmc**, and then click OK to launch the MMC.

4. Click Console, and select Add/Remove Snap-In.

5. In the Add/Remove Snap-In dialog box, click Add.

6. In the Add Standalone Snap-In dialog box, select Exchange System, and then click Add.

7. In the Change Domain Controller dialog box, notice that the default option is for your configuration changes to be sent to Any Writable Domain Controller. It is usually fine to accept the default because the updates will be replicated to all other domain controllers forest-wide. Click OK.

   Why are changes replicated through the entire forest and not just within your own domain?

   _____

   _____

8. In the Add Standalone Snap-In dialog box, click Close.

9. Click OK to close the Add/Remove Snap-In dialog box.

10. Expand your country's Blue Sky Airlines (Exchange) in the console tree.

    What containers are listed under your Exchange organization?

    _____

    _____

    _____

11. Expand the Recipients container.

What containers are listed?

_____

_____

_____

12. Expand the Servers container, and expand your server object.

    Notice that there are two containers: Protocols and First Storage Group.

13. Expand the Protocols container, and then expand all the protocols except the X.400 container. You should see a virtual server listed under each protocol.

▶ **To observe the results after you remove extensions from the Exchange System Manager snap-in**

1. Open the Console menu, and select Add/Remove Snap-In.

2. Click the Extensions tab.

3. From the Snap-Ins That Can Be Extended list box, select Exchange System.

4. Clear the Add All Extensions check box.

    Notice all the available extensions, 19 in all. Without these extensions, your administrative capabilities would be very limited.

5. Clear the Exchange Address Lists, Exchange Address Templates, Exchange Information Store, Exchange Protocols, Exchange Recipient Policies, and Exchange Servers check boxes.

6. Click OK to close the Add/Remove Snap-In dialog box.

7. In the console tree, expand your country's Blue Sky Airlines (Exchange).

    Are you able to expand the Recipients container?

_____

8. Expand the Servers container.

    Are you able to expand your server?

_____

9. Right-click your country's Blue Sky Airlines (Exchange), and select Properties.

10. Select the Display Administrative Groups check box, and then click OK.

11. In the Exchange System Manager dialog box that informs you that you need to exit and restart Microsoft Exchange System Manager to view the results of these changes, click OK.

12. Close your console and select Yes save the console changes.

13. Save the console to your desktop as LAB11.MSC, and then launch LAB11.MSC.

14. Expand Administrative Groups, and then right-click on First Administrative Group.

15. In the shortcut menu, point to New, and then select System Policy Container.

16. Expand the First Administrative Group, and right-click on System Policies.

Are there any options to create a New policy?

_____

▶   **To observe the results after partially reinstalling the extensions for the Exchange System Manager snap-in**

1. Open the Console menu, and select Add/Remove Snap-In.

2. Click the Extensions tab, and then, from the Snap-Ins That Can Be Extended list box, select Exchange System.

3. In the Available Extensions list box, select all the components that were previously deselected.

4. Click OK to close the Add/Remove Snap-In dialog box.

5. In the console tree, expand your country's Blue Sky Airlines (Exchange).

Are you able to expand the Recipients container to see the original subcontainers?

_____

6. Expand Administrative Groups, First Administrative Group, and Servers.

Are you able to expand your server?

_____

7. Expand your server's Protocols container.

Do you see the virtual servers for each of the protocols?

_____

8. Right-click System Policies.

Do you have the option to create a New policy?

_____

9. Open the Console menu, and select Add/Remove Snap-In.

10. From the Snap-Ins That Can Be Extended list box, select Exchange Protocols, and then select the Add All Extensions check box.

11. From the Snap-Ins That Can Be Extended list box, select Exchange Servers, and then select the Add All Extensions check box.

12. Click OK.

13. In the console tree, expand your country's Blue Sky Airlines (Exchange), Administrative Groups, First Administrative Group, and Servers. Expand your server, and then expand Protocols.

Can you expand each of the protocols to see the virtual server?

14. Close the MMC. When asked whether you want to save the console settings to Console1, click No.

What you have observed in this lab is that MMC snap-ins require the proper extensions to be installed to get full administrative functionality. You also observed that some of the extensions even have their own set of extensions. Without all of the required extensions, Exchange System Manager lacks functionality.

Lab 12: Managing Exchange 2000 Server Recipient Objects

Objectives

After completing this lab, you will be able to

- Apply a recipient policy to your user account and view the results.
- Set deleted item retention for your user account.

Note Completing this lab will reinforce your learning from Chapter 13 of the textbook.

Estimated time to complete this lab: 20 minutes

Exercise 1
Applying a Recipient Policy to Your User Account

In this exercise, you will observe your available e-mail addresses and then see how a recipient policy affects your e-mail addresses. You will also configure deleted item retention for your user account.

▶ **To see the results of applying a recipient policy to your user account**

1. Log on to your computer with your user account and password.

2. Launch your Microsoft Management Console (MMC) by clicking on the icon on your desktop.

3. Expand Active Directory Users And Computers, and then expand your domain and select Users.

4. Right-click your user account in the Users container, and then select Properties.

5. Click the Exchange General tab, and then click the Storage Limits button.

6. In the Deleted Item Retention check box, clear the option to Use Mailbox Store Defaults.

7. In the Keep Deleted Items For (Days) text box, type **5**, and then select the Do Not Permanently Delete Items Until The Store Has Been Backed Up check box. Click OK.

Note Exercise 3 in textbook Chapter 13 covers deleted item retention, so this exercise won't go into any more depth than this. These steps are included as part of this exercise just as a second look at how to set up deleted item retention.

---

8. Click the E-Mail Addresses tab.

   What are the available e-mail addresses for your user?

   _____

   _____

   _____

9. Click OK to close the Properties dialog box.

10. Expand your country's Blue Sky Airlines (Exchange).

11. Expand the Recipients container, and then select Recipient Policies.

12. Right-click the Default Policy object, and then select Properties.

    Notice on the General tab that the policy applies to all e-mail nicknames.

13. Click the E-Mail Addresses tab. The address format should correspond to the addresses you recorded in Step 8.

If no other recipient policy exists, the settings of the default recipient policy are used to generate e-mail addresses in Microsoft Exchange 2000 Server. That is why your e-mail addresses correspond to the settings in the Default Policy object.

14. Click OK to close the Default Policy Properties dialog box.

15. Right-click Recipient Policies, point to New, and then select Recipient Policy.

16. Under Name, type **<Your Alias> Recipient Policy** (for example, if your alias is Admin, type Admin Recipient Policy).

17. Click Modify.

18. In the Find Exchange Recipients dialog box, click the Advanced tab.

19. Click the Field menu, point to User, and, from the list of attributes, select Alias.

20. From the Condition list box, select Is (Exactly).

21. Under Value, type your alias name, and then click Add.

22. Click the Find Now button.

23. Confirm that your user account is listed, and then click OK.

24. Read the Warning dialog box about reevaluating proxy addresses, and then click OK.

25. Confirm that your e-mail nickname is in the Filter Rules text box.

26. Click the E-Mail Addresses tab.

27. Select SMTP, and click Edit.

28. Under Address, type **%1s.%g** in front of the @ symbol of the existing SMTP address.

29. Click OK to close the SMTP Address Properties dialog box.

30. Click OK to close the Policy Properties dialog box.

31. Click Yes to update the corresponding recipient e-mail addresses.

32. Right-click the new recipient policy, and select Apply This Policy Now.

Notice that the policy you created has a priority of 1. When multiple policies exist, the recipient policy with the highest priority for any given recipient is applied to that recipient. Once a policy is applied, the policies with lower priorities are ignored. If no policies are found, the Default Policy is applied.

33. Right-click your user account in the Users container in Active Directory Users And Computers, and select Properties.

34. Click the E-Mail Addresses tab.

35. You should now see your new primary address, <1last.first>@<Domain Name>, in addition to your preexisting SMTP address.

Note You might need to wait up to three minutes for the Recipient Update Service to update the change in Active Directory. You can also force the update by right-clicking on the Recipient Update Service and selecting Update Now.

36. Click OK to close the User Properties dialog box.

37. Close your MMC.

Lab 13: Creating a Full-Text Index for an Exchange 2000 Mailbox Store

Objectives

After completing this lab, you will be able to

- Create a full-text index for a mailbox store on your Microsoft Exchange 2000 server.
- Use Microsoft Outlook 2000 to search the mailbox store for keywords in the message subject and message body fields.

Note Completing this lab will help reference your learning from Chapter 14 of the textbook.

Estimated time to complete this lab: 30 minutes

Exercise 1
Creating a Full-Text Index

In this exercise, you will search for messages that contain keywords by using Outlook 2000. Then you will create a full-text index by using Exchange System Manager. After you populate the index, you will search your Inbox using the same keyword and see that the results now include attachments.

▶ **To populate your Inbox**

1. Log on to your computer with your user account and password.

2. Open Windows Explorer, and create a text document named **FULL-TEXT.TXT** that includes the sentence, **This text document will be used to test my full-text index.**

3. Launch Microsoft Outlook 2000.

4. Create a new message to send to yourself that has a blank subject line and FULL-TEXT.TXT as an attachment, and then click Send.

5. Create another new message to send to yourself that has **Full-Text Index Test** in the subject line. Don't include the attachment, but type the following message body: **This line is replacing the text document.** Click Send.

6. After you see that both messages have arrived, open the Outlook 2000 Tools menu and select Advanced Find.

7. In the Advanced Find dialog box, in the Messages tab, type the keyword **index** under Search For The Word(s), and, from the In list box, select Subject Field And Message Body.

8. Click Find Now.

9. What results were returned?

_____

_____

10. Close the Advanced Find dialog box, and exit Outlook.

▶ **To create a full-text index**

1. To create a full-text index, first launch your Microsoft Management Console (MMC) from the desktop.

2. Right-click Blue Sky Airlines (Exchange), select Properties, and confirm that the Display Administrative Groups check box is not selected.

3. Click OK to close the Blue Sky Airlines Properties dialog box. If a dialog box opens telling you that you must exit and restart Exchange System Manager to view the results of your change, do that now.

4. In the console tree, under Servers, expand your server's container, and then expand First Storage Group.

5. Right-click Mailbox Store (<Server Name>), and select Create Full-Text Index.

6. Observe the location of the catalog, and then click OK to accept the default location.

7. Right-click Mailbox Store (<Server Name>), and select Start Full Population.

8. Read the warning, and click Yes to continue.

9. Expand the Mailbox Store object, select the Full-Text Indexing container, and then press F5 to refresh the contents screen.

10. After the Index State value changes from Crawling to Idle, observe the statistics generated by this action.

11. Access the Properties dialog box for your server's mailbox store, and click the Full-Text Indexing tab.

12. Select the This Index Is Currently Available For Searching By Clients check box.

13. Click OK to close the mailbox store's Properties dialog box.

14. Read the warning, and click OK.

15. Close your console.

▶ **To test your full-text index**

1. Launch Outlook.

2. Select Advanced Find from the Tools menu.

3. In the Advanced Find dialog box, in the Messages tab, type the keyword **index** under Search For The Word(s) and, from the In list box, select Subject Field And Message Body.

4. Click Find Now.

   What are the results of your new search? Why is there a difference between the two searches?

   _____

   _____

   _____

5. Close the Advanced Find dialog box.

6. Close Outlook.

Lab 14: Modifying SMTP Settings

Objectives

After completing this lab, you will be able to

- Limit the maximum number of recipients allowed in a single message.
- Create a new Simple Mail Transfer Protocol (SMTP) virtual server.

Note Completing this lab will help reinforce your learning from Chapter 15 of the textbook.

Estimated time to complete this lab: 20 minutes

Exercise 1
Modifying Global Settings
for Your Exchange 2000 Environment

In this exercise, you will restrict the number of recipients that can be included for a single message. You will be modifying a global setting so that your configuration applies to all messages on all the Microsoft Exchange servers in your organization.

▶ **To limit the maximum number of recipients for a single message**

1. Log on to your computer with your user account and password.

2. Launch the Microsoft Management Console (MMC) on your desktop.

3. Expand Exchange System Manager for your organization.

4. Expand Global Settings and display the Properties dialog box for the Message Delivery object.

5. Click the Defaults tab, and, under Recipient Limits, select Maximum (Recipients) and change the number from 5000 to 1.

Note Notice that you have the option to set a limit on both the maximum outgoing message size and the incoming message size. These are global settings, meaning that all users in your organization are affected by the setting. Message size limits can be overwritten on a per-user basis in the user object's Properties dialog box, Exchange General tab.

---

6. Click OK to close the Message Delivery Properties dialog box and minimize your console.

7. Launch Microsoft Outlook.

8. Create a new e-mail message, and address it to the four recipients in your organization.

9. In the Subject line, type **Multiple Recipient Test**, type a short note, and then send the message.

   How many of the recipients received the message? What did the Undeliverable Report tell you?

   _____

   _____

   _____

10. Minimize Outlook, and then restore your MMC.

11. Expand Global Settings, display the Properties dialog box for the Message Delivery object, click the Defaults tab, and then restore the default setting of 5000 for Maximum (Recipients).

12. Click OK to close the Message Delivery Properties dialog box and minimize your console.

13. Click the Outlook icon in your taskbar to restore Outlook, and double-click the message in your Sent Items folder that says Multiple Recipient Test in the Subject line.

14. In the Actions menu, select Resend This Message.

15. Confirm that all the recipients are listed in the To line.

16. On the toolbar, click Options.

17. Select Request A Delivery Receipt For This Message.

18. Click Close.

19. Send the message.

    How many recipients received the message?

    _____

20. Close Outlook.

Exercise 2
Creating and Configuring a
Second SMTP Virtual Server

In this exercise, you will create a second SMTP virtual server. You will observe that you are required to configure a unique IP address/TCP port number combination.

▶ **To create a second SMTP virtual server**

1. Click the MMC icon in your taskbar to restore your MMC console, and expand Exchange System Manager for your organization.

2. Expand the Servers container.

3. Expand your server.

4. Expand Protocols, right-click SMTP, select New, and then select SMTP Virtual Server.

5. In the New SMTP Virtual Server Wizard, on the Welcome wizard screen, type **Second SMTP Virtual Server on <Server Name>** (for example, if your server name is Washington, type Second SMTP Virtual Server on Washington).

6. Click Next.

7. Confirm that the IP address for your server is visible under Select IP Address.

8. Click Finish.

9. If you receive the Warning dialog box regarding your SMTP configuration, read it and then click Yes to confirm that you want to use this IP address.

10. Right-click the new SMTP virtual server.

    Are you able to start the new SMTP virtual server?

    _____

11. Access the Properties dialog box for the new SMTP virtual server, and, in the General tab, select Advanced.

12. Select the IP address for your server, and click Edit.

13. Change the TCP port to **1026**.

14. Click OK three times to exit the SMTP virtual server Properties dialog box.

15. Right-click the new SMTP virtual server, and select Start.

    This time, you should have the Start option available. If not, you might need to refresh your screen.

16. Delete the SMTP virtual server that you just created, and then close your console.

Lab 15: Viewing Link State Information

Objectives

After completing this lab, you will be able to

- Use Exchange System Manager to determine the availability of the connectors in your routing group.
- Use Winroute to examine link state information.

Before You Begin

To complete this lab, you need the following:

- The routing groups created in Chapter 16, Exercise 1 of the textbook, according to the instructor's guidelines.
- The routing Group Connectors (RGCs) created in Chapter 16, Exercise 2 of the textbook, according to the instructor's guidelines.

Topology Required for This Lab

This topology will already be in place in the classroom lab if the class has completed Exercise 1 and Exercise 2 from Chapter 16 of the textbook. Use the following table for server-to-letter association while performing the lab.

Computer Name	Corresponds To
Glasgow	A
Liverpool	B
London	C
Manchester	D
Buenos Aires	A
Lima	B
Rio de Janeiro	C
Santiago	D
Bordeaux	A
Nice	B
Marseille	C
Paris	D
Florence	A
Rome	B
Sicily	C
Venice	D

(continued)

Computer Name	Corresponds To
Capetown	A
Dakar	B
Johannesburg	C
Nairobi	D
Kobe	A
Kyoto	B
Sapporo	C
Tokyo	D
Canberra	A
Melbourne	B
Perth	C
Sydney	D
Antigua	A
Grenada	B
Jamaica	C
Nevis	D

In addition to implementing the topology, check to ensure the following:

- There should be two routing groups, called First Routing Group and Second Routing Group.
- The servers that correspond to the letters A and B in the preceding table should be in First Routing Group, and the servers that correspond to the letters C and D should be in Second Routing Group.
- First Routing Group should be connected to Second Routing Group with a bidirectional RGC.

Note Completing this lab will help reinforce your learning from Chapter 16 of the textbook.

Estimated time to complete this lab: 20 minutes

Exercise 1
Using Available Exchange Tools
to View Link State Information

In this exercise, you will use Exchange System Manager to confirm the availability of messaging connectors that have been installed in your organization. You will also use the Winroute program to examine link state information.

▶ **To view link state information in a fully operational environment**

1. Log on to your computer with your user account and password.

2. Launch your Microsoft Management Console (MMC) from the shortcut created on your desktop.

3. In the console tree, expand your Exchange organization.

4. Expand Administrative Groups, expand First Administrative Group, expand Routing Groups, and then expand the appropriate routing group for your server.

5. Confirm that a Routing Group Connector exists to the other routing group. If one hasn't already been created, you must create one now according to the guidelines in Exercise 2 of the textbook.

6. Expand Tools, and then expand Monitoring and Status.

7. Select the Status container. Confirm that your connector is available.

8. Run C:\LabFiles\Winroute\Winroute.exe.

9. From the File menu, select New Query. Enter your server name in the Server Name text box, and then click OK.

10. Expand RG: <Your Routing Group>. (Expand either First Routing Group or Second Routing Group, whichever is your routing group.)

11. Expand Connectors.

12. Expand your connector, and confirm that the last entry indicates the status is STATE UP.

13. Close Winroute.

14. If your server corresponds to server B, click Start, point to Settings, and then select Network And Dial-Up Connections.

15. Right-click Local Area Connection, and then select Disable to simulate network failure.

16. If your server corresponds to server A, C, or D, launch Microsoft Outlook and send a new message to a recipient on server B.

17. If your server corresponds to server A, C, or D, expand Exchange System Manager, expand Monitoring and Status, and then select the Status container. What do you see? Why?

_____

_____

_____

_____

_____

_____

18. If your server corresponds to server A, C, or D, run C:\LabFiles\ Winroute\Winroute.exe and then select New Query from the File menu.

19. Expand Connectors and confirm that the status of the bridgehead servers and the link state correspond to the results you saw in Exchange System Manager.

20. If your server corresponds to the letter B, click Start, point to Settings, and then select Network And Dial-Up Connections. Right-click Local Area Connection, and then select Enable.

Note You may need to wait a few minutes for this setting to take effect.

21. All students should launch Outlook and send a new message to the other recipients in their organization to confirm that all services have been restored.

22. After all messages are delivered, close Outlook.

23. Close Exchange System Manager.

Lab 16: Creating and Managing Public Folders

Objectives

After completing this lab, you will be able to

- Limit the creation of top-level folders.
- Create a public folder using Exchange System Manager.
- Save a document to a public folder using Microsoft WordPad.
- Create a moderated public folder using Microsoft Outlook 2000.

Note Completing this lab will help reinforce your learning from Chapter 17 of the textbook.

Estimated time to complete this lab: 30 minutes

Exercise 1
Using Exchange System
Manager to Create a Public Folder

You will begin this exercise by restricting who can create top-level folders on your Microsoft Exchange 2000 server. You will then create a mail-enabled public folder using Exchange System Manager and confirm the presence of a directory entry using Active Directory Users And Computers. Finally, you will launch Outlook and experiment with various ways of adding content to your new public folder.

▶ **To limit top-level folder creation**

1. Log on to your computer with your user account and password.

2. Launch the Microsoft Management Console (MMC) that you created on your desktop.

3. Access the Security tab for your organization name in Exchange System Manager.

Note If the Security tab is not available, refer to Chapter 5, Exercise 2, in the textbook to see how to add the required Registry value.

What permissions does the Everyone group have?

_____

_____

4. Remove the group Everyone from the access control list (ACL).

5. Confirm that your user account is listed in the Names box, and then click OK to close the Properties dialog box for your organization.

▶ **To create a mail-enabled public folder using Exchange System Manager and confirm the directory entry in Active Directory Users And Computers**

1. Expand Administrative Groups, expand First Administrative Group, and then select Folders.

2. Right-click Public Folders, point to New, and then select Public Folder.

3. Name the folder **<Server Name> Public Folder** (for example, if your server name is Washington, name the folder Washington Public Folder).

4. Confirm on the Replication tab that this folder will use the public store schedule for the replication interval.

5. On the Limits tab, uncheck Use Public Store Defaults, and then set an age limit for data posted to this public folder to 45 days.

6. Click OK to create the public folder.

7. Right-click your public folder in the Public Folders container, point to All Tasks, and then select Mail Enable.

8. Access the properties for your public folder, and then click the E-Mail Addresses tab to confirm that your public folder has an e-mail address.

   You may need to wait a few minutes to give the Recipient Update Service time to run.

9. Select the Exchange Advanced tab, and then deselect the Hide From Exchange Address Lists check box.

   If your organization is in mixed mode, this check box is deselected by default.

10. Click OK to close the Properties dialog box for your public folder.

11. Expand Active Directory Users And Computers for your server, and then expand your domain name.

12. Select your domain name in Active Directory Users And Computers, and then confirm that Advanced Features is selected in the View menu of your console.

13. Select the Microsoft Exchange System Objects container to confirm that your public folder is listed in the contents pane.

14. Close your console.

▶ **To add content to your new public folder using various methods**

1. Launch Outlook.

2. Expand All Public Folders in the Public Folders container.

   If you don't see the folder list, select Folder List from the View menu.

3. Select your public folder.

4. Double-click any free space in the contents pane to activate a new post form, and notice that your public folder is automatically entered in the Post To field.

5. Type **Post From <Your Account Name>** in the Subject field (for example, if your account name is Administrator, type Post From Administrator).

6. Type a short message, and then click Post from the toolbar.

7. Select Mail Message from the New menu.

8. Click the To option, select your public folder, and then click To.

9. Confirm that your folder is listed in the Message Recipients list box, and then click OK.

10. In the Subject line of the mail message, type **Mail Message From <Your Account Name>**.

11. Type a short message, and then click Send.

Notice that the mail message takes longer to appear in the public folder than the post. Why is that?

_____

_____

_____

12. Minimize Outlook.

13. Click Start, point to the Programs group, point to Accessories, and then select WordPad.

14. Type a short message, and then select Save As from the File menu.

15. Use the Save In list box to drill down to your public folder located in the M:\<Domain Name>\Public Folders folder.

16. Enter **<Your Account Name>.RTF** under File Name, and then click Save.

17. Close WordPad.

18. Restore Outlook.

19. Double-click your document in the contents pane (not the preview pane), and confirm that you can read your message.

20. Close Outlook.

Exercise 2
Creating a Moderated Public
Folder Using Outlook

In this exercise, you will create a public folder, this time using Outlook, and then configure a moderator to approve all posts.

▶ **To create a mailbox for the public folder moderator**

1. Launch the MMC you created on your desktop.

2. Expand Active Directory Users And Computers.

3. Expand your domain, right-click the Users container, and then select User from the New menu.

4. Type **<Server Name>** in the First Name field, and then type **User** in the Last Name field (for example, if your server name is Washington, type Washington in the First Name field and User in the Last Name field).

5. For the User Logon Name, use your server name and the letter *u* (for example, washingtonu).

6. Click Next.

7. Use **password** as the password, click Next twice, and then click Finish to create the mailbox-enabled user.

8. In Active Directory Users And Computers, right-click the Domain Controllers container, select Properties, and then select the Group Policy tab.

9. With Default Domain Controllers Policy selected, click the Edit button.

10. In the Group Policy dialog box, expand Computer Configuration, then Windows Settings, then Security Settings, and then Local Policies; and then select User Rights Assignment.

11. In the Policy list box, double-click Log On Locally, and then add the user account that you just created.

12. Click OK, and then close the Group Policy dialog box.

13. Click OK to close the Domain Controllers Properties dialog box.

14. Close your MMC, and launch Outlook.

15. Right-click All Public Folders in the Public Folders container, and then select New Folder.

16. Name the folder **<Server Name> Classified Ads**, and then click OK.

17. Access the properties for the Classified Ads public folder, and then select Moderated Folder on the Administration tab.

18. Select to set the folder up as a moderated folder.

19. Click the To button, and then double-click the user you just created with your server name.

   You might need to wait for the user to be displayed.

20. Click OK.

21. Click the Add button next to the Moderators box, select the new user, click Add, and then click OK.

22. Confirm that the user is listed as a Moderator, and then click OK to exit the Moderated Folder dialog box.

23. Click OK to close the Properties dialog box for the public folder.

24. Select your Classified Ads folder, and then double-click free space in the contents pane to open a post form.

25. Confirm that the post is to the Classified Ads folder, type **Classified Ad From <Your Account Name>** (for example, if your account name is Administrator, type Classified Ad From Administrator), type a short message, and then click Post.

   Do you see your post in the public folder?

   _____

26. Close all programs, log off as your account, and then log on as the account for your server that you just created.

27. Launch Outlook, and create a messaging profile for the new user.

28. Select Folder List from the View menu.

   Notice that the post to the Classified Ads public folder appears as a message in the moderator's Inbox.

29. Drag and drop the message into the Classified Ads public folder for your server.

30. Select the Classified Ads public folder to view the post, and notice that the original sender's name is still in the From field.

31. Close Outlook.

32. Log off your computer.

Lab 17: The InterOrg Replication Utility

Objectives

After completing this lab, you will be able to

- Install the InterOrg Replication utility.
- Replicate public folder data between organizations.

Note Completing this lab will help reinforce your learning from Chapter 18 of the textbook.

Estimated time to complete this lab: 30 minutes

Exercise 1
Installing and Configuring
the InterOrg Replication Utility

There are five steps to prepare for public folder replication between organizations. In this exercise, your instructor will pair up organizations, and you will configure one server in each organization to be either a publisher or a subscriber. While the publisher and subscriber servers are being configured, the other students in the organization should watch the setup procedure.

▶ **To prepare the publisher server**

Important   This should be performed on one server in the publishing organization.

---

1. Log on to your computer with your user account and password.
2. Launch the Microsoft Management Console (MMC) that you created on your desktop.
3. Using Active Directory Users And Computers, create a mailbox-enabled user with the first name **Replication**, the last name **Agent**, and the logon name **ragent**.
4. Give the user a password of **password**, and select that the password never expires.
5. Right-click the Domain Controllers container, and select Properties. On the Group Policy tab, point to Default Domain Controllers Policy, and select Edit.
6. Under Computer Configuration, expand Windows Settings, expand Security Settings, expand Local Policies, and select User Rights Assignment.
7. Add the Replication Agent account to the rights Act As Part Of The Operating System, Log On As A Service, and Restore Files And Directories.
8. Close the Group Policy window, and select OK.
9. Expand Exchange System Manager.
10. Expand First Administrative Group under the Administrative Groups container.
11. Expand Public Folders under the Folders container.
12. Right-click the public folder for the server that you created in Lab 16, select Properties, click on the Permissions tab, and select Client Permissions.
13. Add the Replication Agent to the access list, and grant the account the Owner role.

Important   If you don't grant the Replication Agent account the Owner role, Default and Anonymous permissions won't be replicated.

---

14. Click OK twice to exit and save your settings for the public folder's Properties dialog box.

15. Right-click the Public Folders container, point to New, and select Public Folder. Type **ExchsyncSecurityFolder** in the Name text box.

16. Click OK to create the public folder.

17. Right-click the ExchsyncSecurityFolder folder, select Properties, click on the Permissions tab, and select Client Permissions.

18. Add the Replication Agent account and change its role to None, leaving the Folder Visible option checked.

19. For the Anonymous and Default accounts, change the roles to None and uncheck the Folder Visible option. Click OK twice.

Note This folder is used by the Replication Service for additional security. A similar folder will also be on the subscriber server.

▶ **To prepare the subscribing server**

Important This should be done on one server in the subscribing organization.

---

1. Log on to your server with your user account and password.

2. Launch the MMC that you created on your desktop.

3. Using Active Directory Users And Computers, create a mailbox-enabled user with the first name **Replication**, the last name **Agent**, and the logon name **ragent**.

4. Give the user a password of **password**, and select that the password never expires.

5. Right-click the Domain Controllers container, and select Properties. On the Group Policy tab, point to Default Domain Controllers Policy, and select Edit.

6. Under Computer Configuration, expand Windows Settings, expand Security Settings, expand Local Policies, and select User Rights Assignment.

7. Add the Replication Agent account to the rights Act As Part Of The Operating System, Log On As A Service, and Restore Files And Directories.

8. Close the Group Policy window, and select OK.

9. Expand Exchange System Manager.

10. Expand First Administrative Group under the Administrative Groups container.

11. Expand Public Folders under the Folders container.

12. Right-click the Public Folders container to create a new top-level folder named for the hierarchy that is being replicated from the publishing organization (for example, if the publishing server is named Glasgow, create a public folder on your server named Glasgow Public Folder).

Note The Replication Service will replicate the entire hierarchy. If there are any subfolders, the Replication Service will create those automatically. If you are replicating multiple hierarchies, you need to create a top-level folder for each one.

13. Click OK to create the public folder.

14. Right-click the new public folder, select Properties, click on the Permissions tab, and select Client Permissions.

15. Add the Replication Agent to the access list, and grant the account the Owner role.

Important If you don't grant the Replication Agent account the Owner role, Default and Anonymous permissions won't be replicated.

16. Click OK twice to exit and save your settings for the public folder's Properties dialog box.

17. Right-click the Public Folders container, point to New, and select Public Folder. Type **ExchsyncSecurityFolder** in the Name text box.

18. Click OK to create the public folder.

19. Right-click the ExchsyncSecurityFolder folder, select Properties, click on the Permissions tab, and click Client Permissions.

20. Add the Replication Agent account and change its role to None, leaving the Folder Visible option checked.

21. For the Anonymous and Default accounts, change the roles to None and clear the Folder Visible option. Click OK twice.

Note This folder is used by the Replication Service for additional security. A similar folder will also be on the publishing server.

▶ **To set up the Replication Agent**

The Replication Agent can be any Microsoft Windows 2000 server with Microsoft Exchange 2000 Server and Microsoft Outlook installed, but typically it is configured on the publisher server. The computer must be in the Windows 2000 domain of the publisher or the subscriber server.

Important This portion of the exercise should be performed on the computer that is configured as the publisher server.

1. Launch Windows Explorer, and create a new folder named **C:\Exchsync**. This is the working directory for the InterOrg Replication utility.

2. Click Start, click Run, type **washington\LabFiles\ExchSync** in the Run dialog box, and copy EXSCFG.EXE (the configuration program) and EXSSRV.EXE (the replication utility) to C:\Exchsync.

▶   **To create a configuration file**

1. Launch EXSCFG.EXE either from the Run dialog box or by double-clicking the file in Windows Explorer.

2. From the Session menu, click Add.

3. In the Add Session dialog box, select Public Folder(s) Replication, and then click OK.

4. In the Title text box, type **Public Folder Replication between <Your Organization> and <Your Partner's Organization>** (for example, if your organization is named United Kingdom Blue Sky Airlines, and your partner's organization is named South America Blue Sky Airlines, type Public Folder Replication between United Kingdom Blue Sky Airlines and South America Blue Sky Airlines).

5. Click Schedule, set replication to repeat every five minutes, and then click OK.

6. In the Publisher Organization group box, type the fully qualified name for your server (for example, Glasgow.bluesky-inc-10.com.uk).

7. In the Mailbox text box, type **Replication Agent**.

8. Click the Advanced button, select Use Alternate NT Account, and type **ragent** for the user name, **password** for the password, and the domain name of your publishing domain for the domain name (for example, if your publishing server name is Glasgow, type bluesky-inc-10.com.uk for the domain name). Click OK.

9. In the Subscriber Organization group box, type the fully qualified name of your partner's server in the Server text box and type **Replication Agent** in the Mailbox text box.

10. Click the Advanced button, select Use Alternate NT Account, and type **ragent** for the user name, **password** for the password, and the domain name of the subscribing domain for the domain name (for example, Bluesky-inc-10.com.sa). Click OK.

11. Click Folder List, click the Logon button for Publisher Public Folders, and then click the Logon button for Subscriber Public Folders.

12. Expand the list of public folders in both the Publisher Public Folders and the Subscriber Public Folders list boxes.

13. Select the public folder for your server in both the Publisher Public Folders and the Subscriber Public Folders list boxes (for example, if your server name is Glasgow, select Glasgow Public Folder in both list boxes).

14. In the field showing the selected folders located below the list boxes, click the arrow to enable bidirectional replication.

15. Confirm that Subfolders is selected, and click the Deletions button.

16. Click Add to add your selection to the file.

17. Click OK twice to add your settings to the configuration file.

18. Save the file as C:\Exchsync\InterOrgSession.esc.

19. Exit Exchange Replication Configuration.

▶ **To set up the Replication Service**

1. Launch C:\exchsync\EXSSRV.EXE.

2. Click Install.

3. Type **<Domain Name>\ragent** for the account name (for example, if your domain name is Bluesky-inc-10.com.uk, type Bluesky-inc-10.com.uk\ragent), and **password** for the password.

4. In the Configuration File group box, browse to the configuration file you created in C:\Exchsync.

5. In the Working Directory group box, browse to C:\Exchsync.

6. Click OK to start the Replication Service.

7. Click Start to start the Exchange Replication Service.

Note If the Replication Service doesn't start, close the Service dialog box and manually start the Exchange Replication Service using the Services Administrative Tool.

▶ **To test your interorganizational public folder replication topology**

Important All students can complete this part of the lab.

---

1. Launch Outlook, and expand All Public Folders under the Public Folders container.

2. Post a message in the publisher public folder with your user name in the Subject field.

   Students should see the posts for their local organization very quickly. It could take up to five minutes to see the posts from the students in the partner organization.

3. After all posts have replicated, stop the Exchange Replication Service on the computer that is configured as the publishing server and confirm that the service is not configured to start automatically at system boot.

4. Close Outlook.

5. Close the MMC.

Lab 18: POP3 Protocol Logging

Objectives

After completing this lab, you will be able to

- Enable protocol logging for the Post Office Protocol version 3 (POP3) Internet protocol using the Registry Editor.
- View the resulting log file using Microsoft Notepad.

Note Completing this lab will help reinforce your learning from Chapter 19 of the textbook.

Estimated time to complete this lab: 20 minutes

Exercise 1
Enabling POP3 Protocol Logging

In this exercise, you will use the Registry Editor to enable protocol logging for the POP3 Internet protocol. You will then access your mail as a POP3 client to create log entries. Using Notepad, you'll view the resulting log files.

▶ **To enable POP3 protocol logging using the Registry Editor**

1. Log on to your computer with your user account and password.

2. On the Start menu, point to Run, and, in the Run dialog box, type **regedt32**. Click OK to open the Registry Editor.

3. Expand HKEY_LOCAL_MACHINE\SYSTEM\CurrentControlSet\Services\ POP3Svc\, and then select Parameters.

4. Double-click POP3 Protocol Log Level, type **5** in the Data text box to set the maximum logging level, and then click OK to accept the default setting Hex.

   Where will the resulting log file be created?

   _____

   Close the Registry Editor.

▶ **To create a log entry**

1. Launch Microsoft Outlook 2000.

2. Address a new message to your user account, and, in the Subject field, type **A simple POP3 Message**.

3. Type a short message in the body, and then click Send.

4. Close Outlook 2000.

5. Launch Microsoft Outlook Express.

6. Open the Tools menu, select Accounts, click the Mail tab, click Add, and then select Mail.

7. In the Your Name dialog page, type your display name, and then click Next.

8. In the Internet E-Mail Address dialog box, type your Simple Mail Transfer Protocol (SMTP) address in the E-Mail Address text box, and then click Next.

9. Confirm that POP3 is selected as your incoming mail server, type your server name under Incoming Mail (POP3, IMAP Or HTTP) Server and Outgoing Mail (SMTP) Server, and then click Next.

10. Confirm that your account name is correct, enter your password, and then click Next.

11. Click Finish to accept the settings, and then close the Internet Accounts dialog box.

12. Press CTRL+M to connect to your server and download messages.

13. Confirm that your message was received.

14. Close Outlook Express.

▶ **To view the resulting log entries**

1. On the Start menu, point to Run, and, in the Run dialog box, type **"C:\Program Files\Exchsrvr\MDBDATA\L0000001.LOG" /n**. Click OK to open the log file using Microsoft Notepad.

2. From the Edit menu, select Find, and, in the Find dialog box under Find What, type **simple**, and then click Find Next.

   Notice that you can view the date and message ID.

3. Press F3 to select the next occurrence of the word "simple."

   Notice that you can determine whom the message is from and to.

4. Press F3 again to see the next occurrence of the word "simple."

   Notice that you can read the body of the message.

5. Close Notepad.

6. On the Start menu, point to Run, and, in the Run dialog box, enter **Regedt32**. Click OK.

7. Expand HKEY_LOCAL_MACHINE\SYSTEM\CurrentControlSet\Services\ POP3Svc\, and select Parameters.

8. Double-click POP3 Protocol Log Level, enter **0** in the Data field to disable logging, and then click OK.

9. Close the Registry Editor.

Lab 19: Using ESEUTIL.EXE
to Read File Header Information

Objectives

After completing this lab, you will be able to

- Use the Extensible Storage Engine (ESE) utility to find the location in your transaction logs that is referenced in the checkpoint file.

- Use the ESE utility to determine the state of your database as consistent or inconsistent.

Note Completing this lab will help reinforce your learning from Chapter 20 of the textbook.

Estimated time to complete this lab: 20 minutes

Exercise 1
Dumping the Checkpoint File Header

In this exercise, you will use ESEUTIL.EXE to dump the header of your checkpoint file. If you perform offline backups, the transaction logs for Microsoft Exchange 2000 Server don't get purged, and eventually you could run out of disk space. Although manually deleting transaction logs is not recommended, sometimes it may be required. You will use the information contained in the checkpoint file header to determine what data has not yet been written to the database before manually deleting transaction logs. Although performing a backup is not included in this exercise, you should always stop your Exchange services and perform a full backup before deleting any log files.

▶   **To dump the header for the checkpoint file**

1. Log on to your computer with your user account and password.

2. Launch Windows Explorer, and expand C:\Program Files\Exchsrvr\Mdbdata to confirm the location of E00.CHK, the checkpoint file for the first storage group.

3. Minimize Windows Explorer.

4. On the Start menu, point to Run, and, in the Run dialog box, type **cmd**. Click OK.

5. At the command prompt, type **cd \Program Files\Exchsrvr\Bin**, and then press ENTER.

6. At the command prompt, type **dir eseutil.exe** and confirm the presence of ESEUTIL.EXE.

7. At the command prompt, type **eseutil /mk "C:\Program Files\ Exchsrvr\Mdbdata\E00.chk">"C:\Program Files\ Exchsrvr\Mdbdata\chk.txt"**, and then press ENTER.

8. After you are returned to the command prompt, minimize CMD.EXE and maximize Windows Explorer.

9. Double-click C:\Program Files\Exchsrvr\Mdbdata\chk.txt to read the header information.

10. Select Checkpoint and notice the series of three numbers in parentheses.

    These numbers represent the log file and the location in the log file that the checkpoint is pointing to. The first number is decimal notation of the log file number. For example, if you have only one transaction log and it is E00.LOG, the checkpoint entry would be 0x1. If you have five transaction logs and the checkpoint file is pointing to the most recent one, or E00.LOG, the entry would be 0x5. Since transaction log files are named using a hexadecimal naming convention, you need to convert the number in the header to hexadecimal.

What is the referenced log file number?

_____

_____

11. Close Microsoft Notepad.

How many total transaction log files are in the Mdbdata folder?

_____

_____

Does the number correspond to the number you recorded from the check-point file header?

_____

_____

What transaction log files can be safely deleted manually?

_____

_____

Exercise 2
Determining the State of the Database

In this exercise, you will use the Extensible Storage Engine (ESE) utility to determine the state of your database. A consistent database is a database file that contains all entries that have been written to a transaction log. An inconsistent database is a database file that does not yet contain all the entries that have been written to a transaction log. An operating Microsoft Exchange 2000 database file is always in an inconsistent state. The only time an Exchange 2000 database file is in a consistent state is when all the services have been shut down properly, thereby flushing all outstanding entries from memory.

▶ **To determine the state of your database file**

1. Using Exchange System Manager, expand Administrative Groups\
First Administrative Group\Servers\<SERVER NAME>\First Storage Group
(for example, if your server name is Washington, expand
Administrative Groups\First Administrative Group\Servers\
WASHINGTON\First Storage Group.)

2. Right-click the Mailbox Store object, and select Dismount Store.

3. Read the warning that states that this action will make the store inaccessible to any user, and then click Yes to continue.

4. Once the process has finished, restore the command window.

5. Confirm that your context is still the bin directory, type **eseutil /m
"C:\Program Files\Exchsrvr\Mdbdata\priv1.edb">"C:\Program Files\
Exchsrvr\Mdbdata\priv.txt"**, and then press ENTER.

   You may need to wait a short while for the process to complete.

6. Close the command window.

7. Expand Windows Explorer, and double-click C:\Program Files\Exchsrvr\
Mdbdata\priv.txt.

8. Look for the entry Last Consistent. Notice that it is the same time that you dismounted the store.

   What is useful about this information?

   _____

   _____

   _____

9. Close Notepad.

10. Close Windows Explorer.

11. Right-click the Mailbox Store object, select Mount Store, and then click OK.

12. Close Exchange System Manager.

Lab 20: Publishing Forms to Forms Libraries

Objectives

After completing this lab, you will be able to

- Create a custom form.
- Publish a form to a folder.
- Publish a form to a personal forms library (PFL).
- Publish a form to an organizational forms library (OFL).

Note Completing this lab will help reinforce your learning from Chapter 21 of the textbook.

Estimated time to complete this lab: 1 hour and 10 minutes

Exercise 1
Publishing Electronic Forms

In this exercise, you will create a custom calendar form and then publish it to each of the three forms libraries. You will test the accessibility of the forms by logging on to your domain with the user account that you created earlier and using Microsoft Outlook 2000 to attempt to open each form.

▶ **To publish a custom calendar form to the folder forms library (FFL)**

1. Log on to your computer with your user account and password.

2. Launch Outlook.

3. Open the Tools menu, point to Forms, and then select Design A Form.

4. In the Design Form dialog box, select Appointment from the Standard Forms Library, and then click Open.

5. Click the (P.2) tab.

6. In the Field Chooser window, click New.

7. In the New Field dialog box, type **Suggested Attire** in the Name box, keep the default setting of Text under Type and Format, and then click OK.

8. Drag your new field from the Field Chooser dialog box onto Page 2 of the Untitled – Appointment (Design) form.

9. Open the Form menu, select Rename Page, type **Attire** under Page Name, and then click OK.

10. Open the Tools menu of the Untitled – Appointment (Design) form, point to Forms, and then click Publish Form.

11. Confirm that the Outlook Folders option is visible under Look In, type **<Your User Names> Appointment Form** under Display Name (for example, if your user name is Administrator, type Administrators Appointment Form), and then click Publish.

12. On the File menu, click Close to close the Untitled – Appointment (Design) dialog box.

13. In the Microsoft Outlook dialog box asking you whether you want to save the changes, click No because for this exercise it isn't necessary to save the form design in a file for future modification.

14. On the Outlook toolbar, right-click your Calendar folder, and then select Properties.

15. Click the General tab, select your appointment form from the When Posting To This Folder, Use list box, and then click OK.

16. Minimize Outlook.

    At this point, where is your custom appointment form physically located?

    _____

17. Launch Microsoft Windows Explorer, and view your forms cache located under C:\Documents and Settings\<User Name>\Local Settings\Application Data\Microsoft\FORMS.

    Do you see your custom appointment form?

    _____

18. Minimize Windows Explorer, and restore Outlook.

19. Select your Calendar folder, and then double-click the appointment area in the contents pane.

20. Type **Company Lunch** in the Subject box, type **Patio Area** in the Location box, and then set the Start and End times from 12:00 P.M. to 1:00 P.M.

21. Select the Attire page, and then type **Casual Friday** as the suggested attire.

22. Click Save And Close, and then confirm that the appointment is on your calendar.

23. Minimize Outlook, restore Windows Explorer, and then refresh the Forms folder by selecting the Forms folder and pressing the F5 key on your keyboard.

    Do you see your custom appointment form? Where is your custom form physically located?

    _____

    _____

    _____

24. Minimize Windows Explorer.

▶ **To publish a form to a personal forms library (PFL)**

1. Restore Outlook.

2. Right-click All Public Folders, and then select New Folder.

3. In the Create New Folder dialog box, type **<Your User Names> Public Calendar** (for example, if your user name is Administrator, type Administrators Public Calendar).

4. Under Folder Contains, select Appointment Items, and then click OK.

    If you receive the dialog box asking, "Do You Want To Add This To Your Outlook Bar?", check the option not to ask you again, and click No.

5. Right-click your folder in All Public Folders, and then select Properties.

6. On the General tab, next to When Posting To This Folder, Use, select Forms from the menu.

7. In the Choose Form dialog box, under Look In, select Standard Forms Library.

   What forms are available?

   _____

8. Again under Look In, select Personal Forms Library.

   What forms are available?

   _____

9. Click Cancel to close the Choose Form dialog box.

10. Click OK to close your Public Folder Properties dialog box.

11. Select your Public Calendar folder under All Public Folders.

12. Double-click the contents pane of your public folder to create a new appointment.

    Does this activate your custom appointment form?

    _____

13. Close the appointment form.

14. Open the Tools menu, select Options, click the Other tab, click Advanced Options, click Custom Forms, and then click Manage Forms.

15. In the Forms Manager dialog box, click the Set button that corresponds to the list box on the left side of the page.

16. Select Folder Forms Library, expand your mailbox, select Calendar, and then click OK.

17. Select your appointment form in the list box.

18. Click the Set button that corresponds to the list box on the right side of the page, select Personal Forms from the Forms Library menu, and then click OK.

19. Click the Copy button to copy the form from your Calendar folder to your personal forms library, and then click Close.

20. Click OK three times to close all dialog boxes.

21. Right-click your public folder under All Public Folders, and then select Properties.

22. On the General tab, next to When Posting To This Form, Use, select Forms from the menu.

23. Under Look In, select Personal Forms Library, select your custom appointment form, and then click Open.

24. Confirm that your custom form is selected in the When Posting To This Folder, Use list box.

25. Click the Forms tab, confirm that Any Form is selected in the Allow These Forms In This Folder group box, and then click OK.

26. Highlight the time from 10:00 to 2:00 in the yellow hourly calendar, and then right-click the highlighted area and select New Appointment.

27. Type **Family Day** in the Subject box, type **The Park** in the Location box, and then confirm the event's start and end times are from 10:00 A.M. to 2:00 P.M.

28. On the Attire tab, type **Play Clothes**, and then click Save And Close.

29. Confirm that the appointment was saved to the public calendar.

30. Close Outlook.

31. Log off as your user account, and log on as **<server name>u**. (For example, if your server name is Washington, log on as washingtonu. This is the user you created in Lab 16.)

32. Launch Outlook.

33. Expand Public Folders, and select All Public Folders.

34. Double-click your public calendar, and then double-click the post for Family Day.

    You may need to wait a short time for the folder to be visible.

    Do you see the Attire page? Why or why not?

    _____

    _____

    _____

35. Close Outlook, and log off as that user.

▶ **To publish a form to the Organizational Library (OFL)**

1. Log on with your user account and password, and launch Outlook.

2. Open the Tools menu, select Options, click the Other tab, click Advanced Options, click Custom Forms, and then click Manage Forms.

3. Click the Set button next to the list box on the left, and then expand the menu under Forms Library.

    What libraries are available?

    _____

4. Click OK, click Close, click OK three more times to exit the Options dialog box, and then close Outlook.

Important Only one student in each organization should complete steps 5 through 9.

---

5. Launch your Microsoft Management Console (MMC) that you saved on your desktop.

6. Expand your country's Blue Sky Airlines (Exchange) organization object, expand Administrative Groups, expand First Administrative Group, and then expand Folders.

7. Right-click Public Folders, and then select View System Folders.

8. Expand Public Folders, right-click EFORMS REGISTRY, point to New, and then click Organizational Form.

9. Type **Organizational Forms Library English** in the Name box, confirm that English (USA) is selected in the E-forms language box, click OK, and then close your MMC.

10. Launch Outlook, open the Tools menu, select Options, click the Other tab, click Advanced Options, click Custom Forms, and then click Manage Forms.

11. Confirm that Organizational Forms Library English is selected for the list box on the left.

12. Confirm that Personal Forms is selected for the list box on the right and that your custom appointment form is in the list box.

13. Select your appointment form, and then click Copy to copy the form to the Organizational Forms Library.

14. Click Close, and then click OK three times to exit the Options dialog box.

15. Open the Public Folders tree, right-click All Public Folders, and then select New Folder.

16. In the Name box, type **<Server Names> Calendar** (for example, if your server name is Washington, type Washingtons Calendar).

17. Under Folder Contains, select Appointment Items, and then click OK.

18. Right-click the public calendar for your server, and then select Properties.

19. Click the General tab, and, from the When Posting To This Folder, Use list box, select Forms.

20. In the Choose Form dialog box, under Look In, select Organizational Forms Library, select your appointment form, and then click Open.

21. Confirm that Any Form is selected on the Forms tab.

22. Click OK to close the properties for your folder.

23. Select the public folder for your server, and then, in the daily calendar, highlight the period between 10:00 A.M. and 2:00 A.M. for tomorrow's date. Right-click the highlighted area, and select New Appointment.

    You may need to wait a short time before your form appears.

24. In the Subject line, type **Company-Wide Meeting**, and then, in the Location text box, type **In the Courtyard**.

25. On the Attire page, type **Business Casual**, and then click Save And Close.

26. Confirm that the appointment appears on the calendar for tomorrow.

27. Close Outlook, and log off your computer.

28. Log on as **<server name>u**, and launch Outlook.

29. Expand All Public Folders, and then select the public calendar for your server.

30. Double-click the post for the Company-Wide Meeting, and then confirm that the Attire page is available.

    If you have an older version in the forms cache, the changes might not show up now. You might need to remove the old version from your forms cache (C:\Documents and Settings\<User Name>\Local Settings\Application Data\Microsoft\FORMS). If you don't see the Local Settings folder in Windows Explorer, select Folder Options from the Tools drop down menu, and on the View tab, select Show Hidden Files And Folders.

31. Select the public calendar that is named after your user account name.

32. Double-click the post for Family Day, and then confirm that you can now see the Attire page.

    Why can you now see the Attire page on the appointment form?

    _____

    _____

    _____

    _____

    _____

33. Close the appointment form, and then close Outlook.

34. Log the user off from your server.

Lab 21: Configuring an Exchange 2000 Server Front End/Back End Topology

Objective

After completing this lab, you will be able to

- Configure a front end server for Microsoft Outlook Web Access (OWA).

Note Completing this lab will help reinforce your learning from Chapter 22 of the textbook.

Estimated time to complete this lab: 15 minutes

Exercise 1
Configuring and Testing a Front End Server

In this exercise, you will work with a partner to establish a front end/back end (FEBE) topology for OWA. After you have configured the front end server, you will test the topology using OWA.

▶   **To configure and test an OWA front end server**

Important This part of the exercise should be performed by Partner A only.

---

1. Log on to your computer with your user account and password.

2. Launch Microsoft Internet Explorer.

3. In the Address box, type **http://<Partner B's Server Name>/ Exchange/<Your Alias>** (for example, if your partner B's server name is Lima, and your alias is Admin, type http://Lima/Exchange/Admin), and then press ENTER.

   Once your mailbox is open, what is the Uniform Resource Locator (URL) that is in the Address box?

   _____

4. Close Internet Explorer.

Important This part of the exercise should be performed by Partner B only.

---

5. Log on to your computer with your user account and password.

6. Launch the Microsoft Management Console (MMC) that you created on your desktop.

7. Expand your country's Blue Sky Airlines, expand Administrative Groups, expand First Administrative Group, and then expand Servers.

8. Right-click your server name, select Properties, click the General tab, click the This Is A Front-End Server check box, and then click OK.

9. Click OK to acknowledge that this server will not become a front end server until the POP, IMAP, and HTTP services are restarted.

10. Click Services in your MMC.

11. Stop and restart each service by individually selecting Microsoft Exchange IMAP4, Microsoft Exchange POP3, and World Wide Web Publishing Service and then clicking the Stop Service and Start Service buttons on your toolbar.

12. Close your MMC.

▶   **To test the new front end/back end topology**

Important This part of the exercise should be performed only by Partner A, but not until all the services have been restarted on Partner B's computer.

---

1. Launch Microsoft Internet Explorer.
2. In the Address box, type **http://<Partner B's Server Name>/Exchange/<Your Alias>**, and then press ENTER.

   Once your mailbox is open, what is the URL that is in the Address box?

   _____

   Why are you seeing a different URL than the one you recorded in step 3 in the first procedure?

   _____

   _____

   _____

   _____

   _____

   _____

   _____

3. Close Internet Explorer.

▶   **To reset the server to a back end server**

Important This part of the procedure should be performed by Partner B only.

---

1. Launch your MMC that you saved on your desktop.
2. Expand your country's Blue Sky Airlines, expand Administrative Groups, expand First Administrative Group, and then expand Servers.
3. Right-click your server name, click the General tab, clear the This Is A Front-End Server check box, and then click OK.
4. Click OK to acknowledge that this server's role will not change until the POP, IMAP, and HTTP services are restarted.
5. Click Start, and, from the Administrative Tools program group, select Services.
6. Stop and restart each service by individually selecting Microsoft Exchange IMAP4, Microsoft Exchange POP3, and World Wide Web Publishing Service and then clicking the Stop Service and Start Service buttons on your toolbar.
7. Close the Services snap-in.

8. Close your MMC.

9. Log off your computer.

Lab 22: Client Access to ExIFS

Objectives

After completing this lab, you will be able to

- Create a network share for a Microsoft Exchange 2000 public folder using the Exchange Installable File System (ExIFS) and then test the share's availability.

- Map a network drive to ExIFS and test its availability.

Note Completing this lab will help reinforce your learning from Chapter 23 of the textbook.

Estimated time to complete this lab: 30 minutes

Exercise 1
Creating a Network Share on
an Exchange 2000 Public Folder Using ExIFS

In this exercise, you will create and access a network share for an Exchange 2000 public folder. You will then reboot your computer to see that the network share no longer exists.

▶   **To create a network share on an Exchange 2000 public folder using ExIFS**

1. Log on to your computer with your user account and password.

2. Launch Microsoft Windows Explorer.

3. Expand My Computer, and then expand Exchange (M drive).

4. Expand the container for your domain, and then expand Public Folders.

5. Right-click the public folder that you created earlier for your server, and then select Properties.

6. On the Sharing tab, select Share This Folder, accept the default share name of the folder, and then click OK.

7. Click Start, point to Run, enter **<Server Name>** in the Run dialog box (for example, if your server name is Washington, type \\Washington), and then click OK.

8. Confirm that the Exchange 2000 public folder is visible in the list of available shared folders on your computer.

9. Close the folder list, close Windows Explorer, and then restart your computer.

10. Log on with your user account and password.

11. Click Start, point to Run, enter **<Server Name>** in the Run dialog box, and then click OK.

    Is your Exchange 2000 public folder still visible in the list of shared folders on your computer?

    _____

    _____

Exercise 2
Creating a Shortcut to a Public Folder Using ExIFS

In this exercise, you will create a network shortcut to an Exchange 2000 public folder in order to have a persistent connection.

▶   **To save a Microsoft Word document to a public folder by creating a mapped drive**

1. Double-click the My Network Places icon on your desktop.

2. In the right pane of the My Network Places window, double-click on Add Network Place.

3. In the Add Network Place Wizard, under Type The Location Of The Network Place, type **http://<server name>/public/<server name> public folder**, (for example, if your server name is Washington, type http://washington/public/washington public folder) and then click Next.

4. In the Completing The Add Network Place Wizard screen, notice that the space in the folder name has been replaced with "%20", and then click Finish.

5. Close the contents window for <Server Name> Public Folder when it appears, and then close My Network Places.

6. Close all programs, and restart your computer.

7. After you log back on to your computer, double-click the My Network Places icon on your desktop to confirm that the shortcut is still there.

8. Close the My Network Places window.

9. Right-click your desktop, select New, and then select Microsoft Word Document.

10. Double-click the document icon, and then type a brief note.

11. Open the File menu, and then select Save As.

12. In the Save As dialog box, select My Network Places.

13. Double-click the shortcut to the public folder on your server, name the file **EXIFS.DOC**, and then click Save.

Note Notice that the file was first rendered (transferred) before being saved to the public folder.

14. Close Microsoft Word.

15. Launch Microsoft Outlook.

16. In the Public Folders container, expand All Public Folders, and then select the public folder for your server.

17. In the contents pane, double-click EXIFS.DOC to read the message in Microsoft Word format.

18. Launch Microsoft Internet Explorer, type **<Server Name>/public** in the Address box, and then select the public folder for your server.

19. In the contents pane, double-click EXIFS.DOC to read the message in Hypertext Markup Language (HTML) format.

20. Close Internet Explorer, and then close Outlook.

Lab 23: Connecting to an Exchange 2000 Server with a Chat Client

Objectives

After completing this lab, you will be able to

- Install Microsoft Chat 2.1.
- Connect to your Microsoft Exchange 2000 server to chat with other people in your organization.

Note Completing this lab will help reinforce your learning from Chapter 25 of the textbook.

Estimated time to complete this lab: 20 minutes

Exercise 1
Installing Chat 2.1

To use your Exchange 2000 server as a Chat server, you are required to use Chat version 2.1 or later. In this exercise, you will install Chat 2.1 so that you can connect to your Exchange 2000 server using the Internet Relay Chat Extension (IRCX) protocol.

▶ **To install Chat 2.1**

1. Click Start, select Run, and, in the Run dialog box, type **C:\LabFiles\Chat\Mschat21.exe**. Click OK to begin the installation.

2. When you see the pop-up box that asks "Install Microsoft Chat 2.1?" click Yes.

3. When presented with the license agreement, click Yes to accept the terms.

4. After the files extract, click OK to install the files in C:\Program Files\ Microsoft Chat.

5. If you receive a dialog box telling you that the folder doesn't exist and asking whether you would like to create it, click Yes.

6. When you see the dialog box that says Thanks For Downloading Microsoft Chat 2.1! Installation Complete!, click OK to close the box.

Exercise 2
Using Chat to Send Real-Time Messages

In this exercise, you will use the Chat 2.1 client software that you just installed to connect to an Exchange 2000 server in your organization and participate in a chat session.

▶   **To use the Chat 2.1 client with Exchange 2000 Server**

1. Click Start, point to Programs, select Internet Explorer, and then select Microsoft Chat.

Note If Microsoft Chat appears in the Programs menu instead of the Microsoft Internet Explorer menu, select Microsoft Chat from the Programs menu.

---

2. In the Chat Connection dialog box, click the Connect tab, and enter in the Server box the IP address of the Exchange 2000 server assigned by your instructor.

3. In the Go To Chat Room box, type the name of the server that corresponds to the IP address entered in the Server box in Step 2.

4. On the Personal Info tab, type your name under Real Name, type your nickname under Nickname, and type your e-mail address under Email Address. If you want, you can also type some information about yourself under Brief Description Of Yourself.

5. On the Character tab, select one of the characters to represent you in the chat room.

6. On the Background tab, select the background you want to see when you are in the chat room.

7. Click OK to close the Chat Connection dialog box.

8. Click OK to close the Message Of The Day dialog box.

9. Type a message in the box located at the bottom of the Microsoft Chat window, and click the button with the Talk bubble located to the right of the box.

Exercise 3
Observing the Results When the Internet Relay Chat Extension (IRCX) Virtual Server Is Stopped on the Exchange 2000 Server

In this exercise, you will stop the IRCX virtual server on the server that is hosting the chat room and observe the effects.

▶ **To observe the effects of stopping the IRCX virtual server**

Important The first five steps should be performed by the student who is at the server that corresponds to the server in step 2 of Exercise 2.

---

1. Launch the Microsoft Management Console (MMC) that you saved on your desktop.
2. Expand Exchange System Manager for your domain, expand Administrative Groups, expand First Administrative Group, expand Servers, and then expand <Server Name>.
3. Expand the Protocols container, right-click IRCX, and select Stop.
4. In the dialog box asking whether you are sure that you want to stop the chat service on your server, and warning you that all user connections to this server will be terminated, click Yes.
5. Close your MMC.

Important All students can complete the remaining steps of the lab.

---

6. Click OK to close the dialog box informing you that you have been disconnected from the server and are now working offline.
7. Click OK to close the dialog box informing you that the system kicked you out of the chat room.
8. Close the chat window.